7

Missing

Missing

Rose Rouse

JOHN BLAKE

Published by John Blake Publishing Ltd,
3 Bramber Court, 2 Bramber Road,
London W14 9PB, England

www.blake.co.uk

First published in hardback in 2008

ISBN: 978 184454 497 4

British Library Cataloguing-in-Publication Data:

A catalogue record for this book is available from the British Library.

Design by www.envydesign.co.uk

Printed in Great Britain by William Clowes, Ltd, Beccles, Suffolk

1 3 5 7 9 10 8 6 4 2

Papers used by John Blake Publishing are natural, recyclable products
made from wood grown in sustainable forests. The manufacturing processes
conform to the environmental regulations of the country of origin.

To all those people
whose loved ones are
still missing.

All days are nights to see till I see thee

WILLIAM SHAKESPEARE
SONNET XLIII

Acknowledgements

Thanks to Wensley Clarkson for showing me the way, and all my friends and family for accepting that I had to say 'No' rather more than they are used to. Thanks to Marlon for countering my Luddite tendencies and simply being there. Also thanks to Brian Cowan and Ross Miller at the charity Missing People, formerly known as the National Missing Persons Helpline, Linda Campbell at the Salvation Army, Samantha Shaw at the Children's Society and Maxine Hamilton Bell at Safe In The City in Manchester, for giving me endless help in my research.

Contents

Introduction

A book about missing people is inevitably an intensely intimate endeavour. I spent three months interviewing mothers, wives, fathers, sons, daughters, brothers and sisters about the loved ones that had disappeared from their lives, including birth parents and some relatives who were found. In one case, I actually interviewed the teenager herself who had run away from home. Writing this book was a daunting task in terms of discovery about people's lives. Missing people disappear for all sorts of reasons – there is no one easy answer. The harsh reality is that, in some cases, people go missing and years later there may still be no explanation.

However, the relatives of the missing always have an unbearable burden to shoulder. These are the very people who generously let me into their heartache, turmoil and grief without making me feel like an intruder. Often, I shared their anguish and determination to carry on searching. At other times, I shared the joy of their reunions. I was, at all times, honoured to be part of their journey.

These are stories of lives that have been shattered by a disappearance but, more than that, these are the tales of relatives who have refused to give up on their missing loved ones. They are still fighting to find out where they are and what happened to them. They are brave, ordinary people whose lives have been irrevocably transformed by circumstances beyond their control. I admire their fortitude. Fate has dealt them an extraordinary and tortuous pathway. They navigate it with grace.

They struggle between searching for the truth and accepting the not knowing. It is an uneasy dynamic. I can only hope that they find some peace and that the stories in this book in a small way acknowledge and affirm both their own lives and those of the missing.

Towards the end of this endeavour, four-year-old Madeleine McCann went missing. The unprecedented coverage of her disappearance has brought deserved attention to the issue and I have included her story because a book about missing people would be incomplete without it.

All stories are true. However, I have had to change some names in order to protect the participants and have indicated where this is the case in the text.

Rose Rouse
February 2008

Chapter One

Madeleine McCann

It's Madeleine McCann's fourth birthday, 12 May 2007. A white card with the words MUMMY, DADDY, SEAN AND AMELIE WILL SEE YOU SOON is tied to a pink balloon and released into the pale blue sky in Leicestershire, not far from the village of Rothley where the McCann family live. Her great uncle, Brian Kennedy, is responsible for releasing that balloon and the 39 others, which fill the sky with their pinkness and their prayers of hope.

The awful truth is that Madeleine isn't actually with her mummy, daddy and twin siblings to celebrate this birthday because she was abducted nine days earlier.

The McCanns are a modern 30-something, middle-class couple with three children. Gerry McCann is a consultant cardiologist; Kate McCann is a GP. At home, they have a nanny because they both work. At the end of April 2007, they flew to the Algarve in Portugal with a group of friends and their children for a two-week holiday. They were all staying in apartments at the Mark Warner Ocean Club Resort at Praia da Luz. Everything was wonderful – the kids had activity clubs, there was a beach nearby, the adults could mix playing with their children and having some time on their own – until the unimaginable happened.

On Thursday, 3 May, the McCanns were eating dinner with their group of eight friends in the resort's tapas restaurant, which Gerry described as 'like having dinner in your garden'. What he meant was that the restaurant was a stone's throw away from their apartment. As usual, the children – Madeleine and the two-year-old twins – were asleep in one of the bedrooms and the McCanns were checking to see that they were fine every half an hour. Just as they had done most evenings. Just as their friends were all doing. They had decided not to use the resort's babysitting service because they didn't want strangers to be involved with caring for their children. They also left the patio doors open, which allowed easy access to the bedroom where the children were all sleeping. Viewed retrospectively, this may appear to be a strange decision to make, but the McCanns thought they were in a secure haven and they considered it less of a fire hazard to leave the doors open.

At 9.30pm, Gerry checked on their three children and found they were all sleeping peacefully. However, at 10pm, when Kate went to check, Madeleine had disappeared. She was no longer in her bed. Gerry and Kate were immediately plunged into a terrifying new universe; a dark, dark place that they had never in their worst nightmares imagined. Their gorgeous little girl – who would become famous through the photograph released showing her blonde and smiling by the swimming pool, radiating happiness on the afternoon of 3 May – was missing and they had no idea where she was. They knew straight away that she had been abducted rather than wandered off on her own.

Within ten minutes, the police were called. Within 24 hours, the entire village, tourists and locals alike, were searching for Madeleine. Sniffer dogs were brought in and the border police with Spain were notified. Yet accusations that the Portuguese police were not doing enough quickly began to appear in the press. The media arrived in Praia da Luz realising that here was a story that would touch the hearts of people everywhere. At this stage, however, not even the journalists foresaw how big Madeleine's story would become. There was something primordial about a stolen child – the story hit us at an emotional level that we can't rationalise away. It encapsulates all our very worst fears.

The McCanns fell into uncharted waters where shock, anguish, fear and guilt were all horribly present. Somehow they managed to function throughout the terrible time. Both parents talked about their terror and despair. 'The worst feeling was helplessness and being completely out of control of anything in terms of getting Madeleine back,' Gerry explains. However, Gerry and Kate managed to garner 'some strength from somewhere'.

Close relatives flew in to support them, including Madeleine's godmothers and Kate's parents, and they started to get thousands of messages of support from people – people that they didn't know, but who cared passionately about their plight. People everywhere took the McCanns into their hearts and poured out feelings of love and empathy. This incredible support was to give the McCanns the strength to stay positive when it would have been so easy to sink into the mire of hopelessness. Of course, they knew that they had stay strong for the twins, plus they were practising Catholics so they drew hugely upon their faith for support too. The church nearby, Nossa Senhora da Luz, became a sanctuary for them and a place where the local community in Praia da Luz could show them love and support as well.

In those first few days, Gerry and Kate appeared on TV to make a brief but heartbreaking appeal to whoever had stolen Madeleine from them. Looking tired and emotionally drained, Kate sat by her husband as he said, 'We would like to say a few words to the person who is with our Madeleine or has been with her. Madeleine is a bright, sunny and caring little girl. She is so special. Please, please do not hurt her. Please do not scare her. Please let us know where to find her or put her in a place of safety and tell somebody about it. We beg you to let Madeleine come home. We need our Madeleine. Sean and Amelie need Madeleine and she needs us. Please give our little girl back. *Por favor, devolva a nossa menina.'*

Family liaison officers from Leicestershire Police flew out to Portugal. Criticism was levelled at the Portuguese police by Madeleine's aunt, Philomena, or Phil, who was Gerry's sister and worked as a teacher. Phil was incensed that the police there seemed to have initially played down the disappearance and hadn't released any details of a suspect. It transpired later that one of the McCann's holiday companions actually saw a man carrying something that seemed to be a child on the evening of Madeleine's abduction, but nothing had been done about it. The Portuguese system of investigation works in a completely different way. In the UK, the police give out as much information as possible in order to recover children quickly. Portuguese police have to abide by their country's law of judicial secrecy, which means virtually no information can be released without risk of jeopardising a trial. This was very frustrating for the McCann family. Days afterwards, Gerry referred to the 'void of information' during the initial period as being very painful for them. There also started to be intimations in the press around this time that this could be an abduction by a paedophile ring.

On Sunday, 6 May, there was a Mother's Day service at the local church and Kate broke down as she expressed her gratitude for the community's support. On the Monday, the Portuguese press reported that the abductors were suspected to be British, then later on the police gave a press conference in which they said Madeleine was being held locally. There were requests for photographs from tourists who might have snapped Madeleine. A couple were reported to have been seen at a petrol station with a blonde girl.

Five days had passed since Madeleine had gone missing and more and more people were becoming involved. In her home village back in Leicestershire, people held a silent vigil with prayers for her safe return, and football superstar Cristiano Ronaldo made a TV appeal. Lots of supposed sightings of Madeleine were coming in and the British ambassador defended the Portuguese police's investigation. After a few days, local searches in the surrounding countryside were wound down so that the investigation could focus on finding suspects. Trauma counsellors were flown out by the holiday company, Mark Warner.

Somehow the McCanns found fortitude and determination in the middle of the chaos. They decided to take charge of the huge media interest in a way which would really help them find Madeleine. They made up their minds that they had to stay positive so that they could get the best results. There was a distinct change in their approach and the change came about because Madeleine had not yet been found. The McCanns became focused on keeping their daughter in the news in the belief that this would increase the likelihood that she would be found. They were desperate, but they channelled their desperation into positive action.

This was something quite new. People in this kind of turmoil usually retreat behind closed doors, feeling too vulnerable to let their intense emotions be on show for the media. The McCanns courageously turned the standard approach on its head. Kate appeared again and again looking wan and distraught, always clutching Madeleine's distinctive cuddly toy cat. She looked as though she was in another universe and she was. They allowed camera crews to follow them around because their mission was to keep their daughter in the headlines in order to find her. There was some criticism of them leaving their children alone but the media were mostly kind and more than willing to participate.

On 11 May, Gerry stated that their intention was 'to leave no stone unturned' in their search for their daughter. The quote headed their official website, www.findmadeleine.com, which went on to attract over 100 million hits within a few weeks. Every parent identified with their desire to find their daughter safe and well. And with their intention to do everything possible to make that happen. David Beckham made a television appeal: 'If you have seen this little girl, please get in touch with the local authorities or police with any genuine information.'

Madeleine's fourth birthday fell nine days after she was snatched from her bed. The evening before there was a poignant late-night vigil in the local church, with 300 people showing their support. The next day, the McCanns took the opportunity to ask everyone to redouble their efforts. Gerry also acknowledged the offers of support being made daily and said it was this 'that keeps us strong and gives us hope. On Madeleine's birthday, please keep looking, please keep praying, please help to bring Madeleine home.' In Leicestershire, pink balloons were released in her honour, while in Portugal her parents took time privately with their twins to mark this special and tragic day. They had bought Madeleine a green doll – green being the colour that symbolises hope in Portugal. Every day, the McCanns could be seen wearing green and yellow somewhere; often, it was Kate's hair ribbons and Gerry's wristbands. They wanted the world to see they were making a demonstration of their feelings of hope.

Friend and fitness instructor Nicola Gill told the press that the McCann's two-year-old twins Sean and Amelie blew kisses at the TV when they saw their sister's face. They were too young to know what was going on but they'd noticed that Madeleine wasn't around. They'd been told that she'd gone on a little trip. It also became apparent that the McCanns were not thinking of returning to England in the near future. 'Today, Madeleine's birthday, was their hardest day,' says Nicola Gill. 'They are not coming home unless Maddy is with them.'

Madeleine's aunt, Philomena, had the brilliant idea of

making a poster that could be downloaded from the internet. Ideas on increasing awareness about the abduction were coming in all the time. Much was made of Madeleine's right eye, in which the black pupil runs into the blue-green iris. It was a distinctive feature clearly visible in photographs and appears on the website and posters. 'We want to make the most of it,' said her mother. 'We know her hair could be cut or dyed.'

Her birthday emphasised the enormity of their loss, but offers of help kept arriving. Billionaire businessman Philip Green offered the use of his private jet plus money. A reward totalling £2.5 million was offered for information leading to her safe return, with Richard Branson, author JK Rowling and Simon Cowell among those contributing. Lawyers flew over from the UK and a fighting fund was started as well. Leicestershire locals tied yellow ribbons and soft toys to the railings of the war memorial in the McCanns' home village of Rothley. This was a spontaneous outpouring of care and concern for Madeleine and the family. The war memorial was a sea of yellow and, comically in this anguish, a giant rabbit reigned over this mass show of support.

Even incoming Prime Minister Gordon Brown expressed his sympathy and, at a later date, apparently contacted the Portuguese police to encourage them to release information about suspects. They did finally release the description of a suspect – although they got the height wrong – and then arrested a local English expat, 33-year-old Robert Murat. Hysterical newspaper headlines followed and the house that he shared with his mother was searched and a computer removed. Despite all the speculation, he was released without charge.

On 16 May, Gerry and Kate – who had been constantly

photographed and occupying front pages, whether with pictures of them running, or playing with the twins – took questions from journalists for the first time. The information that they were keen to impart was that they believed their daughter to be alive, safe, well and looked after. It was crystal-clear that the Madeleine case was receiving unprecedented coverage, serving also to highlight how little coverage there is for the hundreds of other less media-friendly cases of missing teenagers and adults. The hope was that Madeleine's case would bring more attention to the whole issue of missing people. 'This case has raised awareness that "missing" is a social issue that could affect every one of us,' said Paul Tuohy, the chief executive of Missing People. 'We hope it has changed public perceptions. We now need the public to show support for all missing people and those left behind.'

The McCanns drew enormous wells of strength from their own prayers and those of others, as well as from the support of the media and the caring messages via the internet. They visited Portugal's most important shrine, Fatima, where there was a special prayer service for Madeleine. Kate and Gerry were showered with hugs and kisses from the hundreds of ordinary people at the shrine. So many people shared their pain and showed they care – it was almost overwhelming. They spent an hour in one of the chapels praying on their own. Afterwards, people burst into spontaneous applause. They can't help but be touched, but the reality is it was the 20th day that their darling daughter had been missing and, despite all the phone calls to the police and the supposed sightings, she still hadn't been found.

On 25 May, Gerry and Kate gave their first media interview.

Obviously striving to control their turbulent emotions and anguish, they admitted they felt guilty that they weren't with her when she was abducted. 'No one will ever feel as guilty as we do,' they confessed, adding that they were also aware that thousands of parents also leave their children in similar circumstances. They told the interviewer that Madeleine was an extroverted, vivacious and lovely little girl who they believed will be found safe and well. They also said the holiday had been idyllic before Madeleine was taken and that she'd been having great fun with her twin brother and sister. 'She might look like Kate,' says Gerry, 'but in terms of personality, she is more of a McCann. She is very fiery and often a little ringleader in the nursery and with her friends.'

They also talked about how difficult it was to have little information from the police in the first 48 hours. 'It took us back to the darkest places, where we didn't want to be and which ultimately didn't help us,' said Gerry. He talked about being 'almost non-functioning' for that period of time, but that communication channels had opened up since then. 'Certainly, at the moment, we are happy about how information is conveyed to us,' he said. They also added that it had helped tremendously when they had started to take control of the publicity around the case. Again, they stressed their thanks to all the people that they didn't know who were doing so much to help. And they urged people to get in touch with information. 'We believe the public will hold the key,' he said. 'Someone knows something.'

British police from the Child Exploitation and Online Protection Agency had received more than 500 images, which they were cross-referencing against a database of pictures of UK paedophiles. There were reports of a sighting of a little girl seen in Morocco asking when she could see her mummy, as well as those reports of the couple at a petrol station with a little blonde girl. There was information but no clear leads. Behind the scenes, there was a lot of police activity, but the McCanns were having to plan how to find Madeleine and support themselves, not to mention their families and close friends.

They were invited to go to the Vatican and have an audience with the Pope. Being such committed Catholics, they seized the chance to receive such an important blessing and reinforcement of their own faith that Madeleine was still alive. They also realised that the world coverage of them in Rome would focus fresh attention on Madeleine's story. Gerry and Kate took Philip Green's offer of a private jet even though they had to leave the twins for the first time. It was difficult for them to separate, although the twins were with relatives.

In the Vatican, they were seated in the front line at the service and received a personal prayer and meeting with the Pope. They were very moved by the encounter. The Pope showed recognition when he saw their faces and he said he would pray to help them sustain their hope and determination to find Madeleine. He put his hand on the photo of Madeleine. It was 30 May, 26 days after their precious daughter's disappearance, and they needed to gather strength all the time to nurture their determination to find her. In other circumstances, they would have relished seeing the Pope in such a private way, but their agony was too much for it to be a pleasure. They did, however, receive a tremendous lift in spirits from this religious experience.

The McCanns decided to extend their campaigning plans to

cover other countries. There was a distinct feeling that Madeleine would have been taken out of Portugal very quickly. They set on visiting various places where her abductors might have taken her or where people might have returned after having been on holiday in Praia da Luz and seen something of relevance without realising it. They made their minds up to go to Spain, Germany, the Netherlands and Morocco in order to increase awareness and to try to find out any additional information. Gerry stressed that it was not a tour but a series of brief visits with a purpose. It was a strange case for the public, who had never witnessed parents of the missing with such enormous resources at their disposal. It felt as if the search might turn into a global media circus. However, both parents maintained a very level-headed approach throughout.

They visited Spain straight after Rome and gave a press conference urging people to download pictures of Madeleine and share any information they had. The family of a seven-year-old boy who was abducted a couple of months earlier in Gran Canaria handed the McCanns a letter of support. Encouraged by the Spanish response to their search, they returned to the Algarve and their twins feeling as though the Spanish embraced them as if they were their own countrymen.

On the day marking a month since Madeleine's disappearance, there was a special service in Praia da Luz. Kate broke down when a young Portuguese girl kissed her on the cheek as the congregation exchanged signs of peace. The Igreja Nossa Senhora da Luz church has been their sanctuary and the place local people have shown them enormous amounts of care, concern and love. Again and again, the McCanns returned to this church for strength and the courage to carry on. 'It is incredibly difficult not having Madeleine here,' said Gerry, 'as every day and week becomes a month. We still believe she is out there and alive, and we remain positive and determined that we will find her with everyone's help.'

Madeleine's picture was also screened during the FA Cup final to an estimated audience of 500 million. Gordon Brown wore a yellow ribbon to demonstrate his solidarity. She has also been the cover story on scores of publications, including *People* magazine in the USA, where Oprah Winfrey invited the McCanns to appear on her talk show.

On 5 June, they appeared on *Crimewatch* in the UK, holding a pair of pink pajamas adorned with pictures of Eeyore the donkey from *Winnie the Pooh*, clothes identical to the ones that Madeleine was wearing when she disappeared. Kate said she hoped that Madeleine had been taken by someone who was 'sad' as opposed to 'bad' and who wouldn't harm her. Gerry went on to give a detailed description of the suspect – seen by their friend – who had been observed carrying what was thought to be a child on the night that Madeleine disappeared. The suspect was about 35 with dark hair parted at the side and longer at the back. He wore a dark jacket.

They also appeared on TV in Berlin and were asked as part of the open interview by German journalists what they thought about the fact that more people seemed to be pointing the finger at them for the abduction. Slightly incredulous, Gerry and Kate calmly defended themselves but the accusation made headlines all over the UK. They repeated that it would only take one phone call for them to find their little girl, and encouraged people to do so. They then went on to Amsterdam to do a press conference there as well.

The Portuguese police gave the parents an update on the investigation. There were reports about DNA tests and forensic results but no conclusive news. The UK police reported 1,000 sightings and 15,000 calls.

It seemed that Gerry and Kate accepted the hunt for Madeleine might be lengthy. They intended to appoint a long-term campaign manager to maintain awareness of Madeleine's plight. They also spoke of Madeleine's abduction as being like a 'bereavement', or like 'being diagnosed with cancer', and admitted they had been forced to face the fear that their daughter might be dead. 'There are a lot of mixed emotions and anger is one of them,' said Gerry. But if you give up hope, you are basically saying she is dead. No parent would do that.'

Gerry and Kate organised some quiet time for themselves and the twins away from the glare of the media. Now they had a balancing act to achieve – keeping the semblance of normal family life going for the twins, while maintaining a focus on Madeleine until she was found. They scaled down their activities, leaving them time to expend some energy on how to develop the campaign effectively in the future.

On 22 June, balloons were released in countries all over the world from Afghanistan to South Africa to mark the 50th day of Madeleine's disappearance. Hope was always the focus, but the police investigation and media attention brought all sorts of different difficulties and pain over the next few weeks.

Police dug up the garden belonging to the mother of suspect Robert Murat but nothing was found to link the man who had been the subject of media speculation. British detectives had flown over to join the investigation and the most disturbing development for Gerry and Kate was their discovery of blood traces in the apartment. It was flown back to the UK to undergo DNA tests.

Unfortunately, the Portuguese press leapt to the wild conclusion that Madeleine was killed there rather than abducted. Gerry and Kate found themselves the subjects of a heartless and absurd smear campaign in Portugal where they and their holiday companions were accused of being involved in Madeleine's death. This caused unnecessary extra anguish for the devastated parents.

Amid all the cruel innuendos and crazy speculation, Gerry and Kate turned again to their faith for strength. On 11 August, to mark the 100th day of Madeleine's disappearance, they did a series of press interviews and there was an hour-long service at Nossa Senhora da Luz. Locals and holidaymakers wore the now familiar yellow and green of hope, and Kate stood up and spoke movingly about her missing daughter. 'Every day feels so hard without Madeleine. I could talk all day about how wonderful, how precious Madeleine is, but suffice to say we all miss her so much and our lives aren't complete without Madeleine.'

They left the church to depressing news from the police. For the first time, the Portuguese officer leading the hunt for Madeleine admitted she could be dead. He was referring to the specks of blood found in the apartment.

No-one could possibly have foreseen what would happen to the McCanns over the next month. As reports of DNA investigations were leaked to the press, the McCanns themselves became the subject of intense scrutiny and accusation. Not just in Portugal, but in the UK as well.

On 6 September, Kate was questioned for 11 hours in Portugal and then named as an *arguido* (which translates as somewhere between a crucial witness and a suspect). the next day, Gerry was questioned for eight hours then named an *arguido* himself. It was reported that the McCanns had been under 24-hour surveillance for the previous month. The newspapers in the UK and abroad were full of speculation that Kate was shortly to be charged for Madeleine's murder and that it was suspected that she accidentally gave Madeleine an overdose of sedatives.

The world seemed to have gone insane. What parents would put themselves through this kind of media circus if they had made this kind of tragic mistake? There were endless media reports about Madeleine's DNA having been found under a rug in the back of the McCann's Renault Scenic hire car (which they had hired 25 days after Madeleine's disappearance). The implication was that they had used this car to dispose of her body. There were also reports of sniffer dogs reacting to the car, which implied that it had contained a dead body. In fact, there was a feeding frenzy of hysterical headlines.

In the midst of this media madness, the McCanns flew home to Rothley. At last, they were home. Without Madeleine, but at least they could start to return to some kind of normality with the twins.

Within four months, the McCanns had been transformed from the tragic parents of a beautiful, abducted daughter to her supposed murderers and the unprecedented coverage of this case started to show its dark side. Like celebrities who walk that difficult tightrope between adoration and decimation, the McCanns attracted the baying hounds of destruction. Indeed, Gerry announced as they returned, 'We've been stitched up.'

The McCanns have now hired an impressive legal team to

clear their names, as well as private detectives to keep looking for Madeleine. Richard Branson has stuck his neck out and put £100,000 into their legal fighting fund. By 20 September, the tide was turning yet again, this time in favour of the McCanns. The Portuguese admitted there was no new evidence that warranted re-interviewing them.

A new spokesman, Clarence Mitchell – who initially provided consular support – has left his job to join the McCann team because he believes so passionately in their innocence. Meanwhile, the McCanns are trying to refocus their 'Find Madeleine' campaign. They refuse to give up hope even now when logic is against it. They are Madeleine's parents and, as long as there is no proof of her death, they will go on believing she is alive.

No doubt the headlines will continue. In the meantime, little Madeleine's disappearance has touched so many different people in so many different places.

Gerry and Kate are hoping the spotlight will stay on their daughter, but will also reach out to include other missing children. They are well aware that they are not the only ones whose loved one is missing.

Chapter Two

I Miss My Sweet, Gorgeous Son

Jo Gibson Clark has had more heartbreak in the last two and a half years than any mother should experience, ever. Her gorgeous, charming, adventurous 19-year-old son, Eddie, went missing on 24 October 2004, in Cambodia. It should never have happened. On that date, Eddie was supposed to be at lectures as part of his joint honours degree in International Management and Asian-Pacific Studies at Leeds University.

Jo lives in Hove with her second husband, Tony Clark, and had two other sons, Elliott, 28, and Max, 18, by her first husband, Mike Gibson. Mike was also Eddie's father and, although the parents split up when Eddie was just 11, they remained on good terms and Mike would often pop over for Sunday lunch. Jo drove Eddie up to Leeds on 15 September 2004. 'He seemed keen to get on with his degree,' she says. 'He'd done a gap year with friends and they'd travelled to Australia, Thailand, Burma, Laos and Cambodia, so Eddie seemed absolutely ready to study and said he valued his education. He appeared to be very keen to start his new course. I was really happy for him.'

Ever entrepreneurial, Eddie had managed at the last minute to talk his way into a university room right next to one of his old friends from Brighton, Josh. That really pleased him. And his mother. The room wasn't great but it wasn't too bad either. 'It smelt like a hospital in there,' says Jo. 'And it had bars on the window, which I thought he'd find difficult to cope with, but we went out and bought rugs, throws, candles and lamps to give it a homely feel and he seemed fine. Josh, Eddie, Max and I all went out for a nice meal together and I kissed him goodbye, convinced that he was starting an exciting new phase of his life.' That was to be Jo's last face-to-face encounter with her lovely son.

Eddie had blond, spiky hair and was six feet tall. Not surprisingly, he was always a firm favourite with the girls and he was smart too, with A grades in his A-levels. Definitely a bit of a star. He seemed to have led a charmed existence and Jo fully expected him to continue in the same manner. However, he did have a streak of dare devil in him even when he was a young boy and perhaps that willingness to take risks caught up with him. 'How could I have possibly guessed that I'd never see him again?' she asks, still in a state of confusion about how and why he disappeared.

For the first week at university, Eddie seemed fine. He phoned both his parents regularly and told them all the news about fresher's week and Leeds. They didn't suspect anything was wrong at all. 'He'd signed up to do sky-diving, which he loved,' she says, 'and joined a football team. He seemed contented and to be settling in.'

But the true picture wasn't as clear as that. In fact, Eddie seemed to be hiding some deep confusion. At some point between 15 September and 4 October 2004, Eddie changed his mind about his course and being at university. He decided it wasn't for him. But he kept this information to himself. He might have been afraid that his parents would feel he was letting them down, and he was never good at facing that kind of situation. He didn't even tell his old friend Josh. 'He wasn't naturally secretive,' says Jo, 'but he didn't like having to explain his actions or confronting things. He'd rather approach tricky situations like this sideways rather than head on. Also, once he'd decided on a course of action, he was single minded in his determination to carry it out. He'd always been like that.'

In fact, there were a couple of clues that all was not well just before 4 October, the date that Eddie took a flight to Bangkok via Dubai with £3,000 from his bank account. On Friday, 1 October, at 10.30pm, which was quite late for him to ring, he called his mother. 'He said, "I just want to hear your voice, Mum," which was very unusual,' she said. 'I was touched but I was also surprised.'

Then on Sunday, 3 October, she had another call from him. 'He said, "Mum, I'm really unhappy about my course and I'm not sure what to do." I told him not to panic, that it would all sort itself out. I knew he was sensible and I wasn't really worried. I thought he'd work it out,' she says. He rang again later that day and said that he was changing his course from International Management to Business and that he'd talked to the right professor about this. He added that his battery on his mobile was low, which meant he wouldn't be phoning home for a few days.

At this point, Jo wasn't concerned because she thought he'd organised his change of course and that he was OK. 'He was always so capable,' she says. 'I expected him to be OK. What I didn't realise was that he'd already made up his mind to go back to Cambodia.' Eddie was evidently in some turmoil about this decision. Much later, Jo actually discovered that he had bought a ticket to Bangkok the day before he called and travelled down to Heathrow. At the last minute, he'd changed his mind again and gone back to Leeds. This was when he'd talked to his mother, but hadn't told her the full extent of his worries and plans. He was probably thinking that he was creating disappointment for his family and couldn't face that.

On the Monday, Eddie bought another ticket and this time he got on the plane. Later, his parents found out that he'd stayed in Bangkok for a couple of days before crossing the border into Cambodia on 9 October. 'Now I wonder if he was setting up a bank account,' says Jo. 'He was sensible with money. I can't imagine him walking around with £3,000 in his pocket. That's one of the things we're still trying to investigate – what exactly Eddie did with his money.'

Eddie had been captivated by Cambodia during his gap year. With a group of school friends, he went to Australia, then to Thailand, Laos and Burma, but it was Cambodia that captured his heart. The combination of their tragic history – 1.7 million Cambodians were killed by the terrible Khmer Rouge between 1975 and 1979 in the infamous 'killing fields' – the poverty and the kindness of the people he met had a profound effect on him.

'He met people who had no relatives because they'd all been killed by the Pol Pot regime and who had no money, yet Eddie thought they seemed much happier than people in the West,' says Jo. 'That made him question our value system here. He came back and threw out his Armani and Boss clothes. He didn't see the need for them any more. He walked around in T-shirts, flip flops and shorts just like he'd worn over there. He didn't like the greed he saw in the West.'

Finally, he seemed to have made the decision that it was more important for him to experience more of this kind of non-materialistic existence in Cambodia than to take his university degree course. He had a return flight booked for 1 November so he was planning to be away at least a month. Not that his family realised that any of this was happening. They thought that Eddie was happily ensconced in his hall of residence in Leeds. Jo did think it was a little strange that Eddie missed his brother Max's birthday on that first Wednesday. He sent a card and a present but he didn't phone. She tried to ring his mobile but there was no answer. She rang Josh and asked if he'd seen Eddie and he said he thought he'd seen him somewhere but Jo wasn't reassured.

By the end of the week, Jo was in a terrible state. 'I rang the university and asked them to break into his room,' she says. 'I was imagining that Eddie was lying dead in a pool of blood. Finally, they did get in and Josh reported that everything was still there except for a little satchel, a black holdall, his passport and money. Then, I knew that he'd probably gone abroad. I was incredibly shocked and worried.'

She rang the police, who were reluctant to do anything because Eddie was 18 and therefore free to make his own decisions. Then she phoned Missing People, who advised her to phone the Foreign Office to check if he'd left the country. It turned out that Eddie had mentioned to a couple of friends in Hove that he wanted to go back to the Far East, but none of them had taken him seriously.

Jo also phoned around the hospitals in Leeds, checking to see if Eddie was lying there injured. By 15 October, the family knew that Eddie had crossed the border into Cambodia. She turned all her attention back to the police, trying to get them to find out more information. But they weren't prepared to do anything. Eddie had made the decision to go and that was that as far as they were concerned. 'Mike wasn't as worried as me at this stage,' she says. 'He thought it was just Eddie doing his own thing.'

Finally, on 20 October, Jo got an email from Eddie in Phnom Penh. 'I felt the happiest I've ever been,' she says. 'I was so excited, so relieved and so incredulous all at once. I'd been emailing him three or four times a day, and the rest of the family and friends had been too, so he must have had at least a hundred emails. He apologised for going off without telling us and explained that university just wasn't for him. He said he was coming back on 1 November and told me not to worry. He also said I was the best mum in the world and he was looking forward to seeing us all again. Then he made it clear that he wasn't going to open his emails again because he wanted "to clear my head and decide what to do with the next three years of my life".'

Eddie gave her the impression that this was something he had to go through on his own. Of course, Jo was overjoyed to hear from her son, but she also wanted to let him know what she'd been going through. She emailed him back. 'Oh my God, promise you will never do that again. You have no idea how worried I've been and what thoughts have been going through my mind. I can't wait to see you. I'm not angry with you and it doesn't matter about university. You are bright and everything will be fine.' Jo is not sure whether Eddie ever read it.

She received one more email four days later. 'He said he was definitely coming home on 1 November,' she says, 'and he was ready to come because he'd seen enough of the poverty and deprivation over there.' It was enough to reassure her and convince her. Jo was looking forward to having her son home in her arms again. Both parents were determined to be there at Heathrow when Eddie got off that flight.

They drove up together from Sussex. Jo was so excited about seeing and holding her son after so much anxiety over his safety. At 7.15pm, travellers started to come through from the flight from Bangkok. Jo and Mike were right in the front of the exit doors ready to give him a huge welcome. But ten minutes later there were only a few stragglers with backpacks left. And none of them was their son. The doors shut and these two parents had to face the nightmare reality that Eddie was not there. He had not come back.

'I felt torn apart,' says Jo. 'My emotions just went into overdrive. Waves of shock and terror ripped through me.' She ran over to the British Airways desk and asked them to check whether Eddie had boarded the flight in Bangkok. She was allowed to know, but only because she worked as a member of British Airways ground staff and was able to show them her security pass. They confirmed that Eddie hadn't got on the plane. Jo had thought her living hell was about to end – tragically, it was just about to start.

Jo later confessed that, on the way to the airport, she'd had a faint suspicion that Eddie wouldn't arrive, while Mike was still convinced that Eddie would be back in his own time. At home, Jo couldn't hold back the pain and anger any longer. She wrote Eddie an email that was incandescent with rage. It read, 'I can't believe the pain you are putting us through. We were so looking forward to seeing you. I can't believe you would be so selfish. You don't know what it is like to be a parent and go through this. Make contact with us. Let me know you're OK.'

Naturally, Jo was absolutely desperate to hear from her missing son. She wanted to tell him everything she was feeling and how hurt she was. She wanted to communicate with him and hear what was happening to her boy. But in fact, she never heard another word from Eddie. The next day, feeling terribly guilty, she sent him another email apologising. Meanwhile, Mike was still confident that Eddie would come home when he was ready. 'Remember,' he would say, 'Ed hates fuss and confrontation, and having to explain his actions. He'll be home in his own time.'

To keep her mind occupied, Jo busied herself with activities connected to finding Eddie. She phoned prisons in Thailand to see if he could be there – although she is quick to point out that she always warned Eddie about people planting drugs on him and that he was never interested in drugs. She also phoned the Buddhist centres in Cambodia. 'I thought Eddie might have decided to clear his head there,' she explains. 'I even found a professor who specialised in Buddhism who was going there. He said he'd check them out for me but on his return he told me that it was very unlikely that Eddie was in that sort of centre. Not many Westerners can take that sort of regime, which includes cleaning rotas and being up at 4am, plus they also only speak Cambodian.

Jo also sent out a chain global email saying she was looking for her son and asking if anyone had seen him. She got emails back but no real news. Eddie had kept detailed dairies of his gap year, so Jo read them now, looking for names of hotels in Cambodia and then emailing them to see if Eddie had stayed there recently. She was incredibly industrious. But she didn't have any luck.

Christmas 2004 was approaching and they were all convinced that Eddie wouldn't miss it. But, horribly, there was no word from him. Now his father and eldest brother Elliott decided to take action and flew out to Cambodia to try to find him. 'It was a dreadful Christmas,' says Jo. 'We had my mother over and she's eighty-seven. We hadn't told her about Eddie because we didn't want to worry her. But now I had to tell her. She took it better than I thought she was going to, but I suppose she lived through two wars when people went missing regularly. Telling her somehow made it official. It made me feel in total despair.'

Unbelievably, Mike and Elliott arrived in Phnom Penh and the tsunami happened on the same day. All the police officials with whom they had wanted to find and discuss Eddie's disappearance had been diverted to Vietnam and Thailand. However, they did manage to put 'missing' posters up everywhere.

'From the diaries, I could see Eddie had had a relationship with a girl in Bangkok. Mike and Elliott managed to find her but they discovered he hadn't gone back to visit her this time,' she says. 'But she started to help us too.' They talked to bar owners and went down to beaches where travellers hang out. Cambodian girls would say they'd seen him, but these sightings all proved to be untrue. Yet Mike and Elliott came back still positive, still thinking he was there somewhere, they just hadn't found him yet.

Unable to stay at home when the others had been in the country where Eddie had gone missing, three weeks later, Jo and Tony flew to Phnom Penh. They met up with the British embassy's vice consul who explained that Westerners would often get picked up by 'taxi' girls, who would totally look after them in return for being financially supported. 'He said Westerners often occupied this unreal, bubble world, which was lovely, very peaceful and cheap. Then there were the local drugs like yabba, an opium derivative, which would keep them permanently high. Lots of Westerners apparently end up living out here for ten years just to escape life at home,' says Jo. Presumably, the embassy official was suggesting that Eddie could have made that choice too.

However, Jo couldn't see Eddie getting into drugs. He liked being in control too much, plus he was really into his health. 'Unlike my other boys, he was always shopping for fruit and vegetables,' she said. 'He really cared what he put in his mouth.' Jo had an aim on her trip and it was to get on TV and in the newspapers over there. 'I wanted as many people as possible to be aware that Eddie was missing,' she says.

Unlike her son, Jo hated Cambodia. 'It is the worst place I've ever been to,' she says. 'I saw all the pretty girls there and the beaches, but underneath there is such a basic need to survive that people will do anything for money. There is also a feeling of immorality that maybe came from the Pol Pot era. It feels as though people will do anything, however ruthless, to survive. We went to one of the backpacker's hangouts and it was horrific, filthy and full of drug addicts – it was vile. We looked to see if Eddie's name was on the register, but it wasn't. I was so shocked by these places. Parents would never let their children go there if they knew what they were like.'

Jo managed to get a lot of coverage on TV, radio and in the newspapers. Expats offered help, Cambodians also came forth and offered information, but Jo was only too aware that the latter were often just interested in the cash being offered. One Cambodian man said to her, disturbingly, 'You realise that people get killed here for fifty dollars and the killers simply bury the bodies.' The horror of the possibilities in a country with such a corrupt underbelly hit her, but Jo refused to give up. 'I was crying, I felt so sick,' she says. 'We also tried police stations, which was another horrible experience. The police there have gold teeth and crisp, green uniforms, but they don't inspire any confidence. Basically, they won't do anything without being paid. Everyone wants to be paid. It's very demoralising.'

She did find a man called George who did sincerely offer to help. He was an American lawyer who put posters up and contacted hotels to see if Eddie had been there. There was also Gareth, a lovely Welsh man who Jo happened to ask for directions when she was walking along the beach. He recognised her voice because he'd heard her do a radio interview there about Eddie. 'Are you Eddie Gibson's mum?' he said immediately.

'I was so excited that he knew who I was, it made me feel hopeful. He has turned into a friend and helped out a lot,' she says.

But mostly she was approached by shifty characters who were obviously after money. Which made her search even more distressing. There was one man who was Israeli and, she says, looked like Colonel Gaddafi. He promised he'd find Eddie, but she didn't even consider taking him on. 'I was still going to bars and half expecting Eddie to be sitting there,' she says.

Leaving Cambodia without any concrete news about Eddie was extremely tough for Jo. 'I was so sad,' she says, fighting back the tears. 'I felt as though I was leaving my Eddie there. That was so difficult emotionally.'

Back home, she kept getting emails. Most were from Cambodians claiming to have news of her son, but they were obviously lying. They were all insisting, of course, that they needed money to help. Then Jo received an email from a Korean girl called Constance who was living in Phnom Penh. She was a friend of a Cambodian girl called Ami, who had apparently been having a relationship in October with Eddie. At last, this was the possibility of a real breakthrough. Jo allowed herself to become a little hopeful of finding out the truth.

And this piece of information turned out to be real. It transpired that Eddie had been staying with Ami from 9–24 October. The lovely Welshman, George, was duly dispatched to find Constance and to try to locate Ami through her. He did. Eddie had, it turned out, met Ami during his gap year at a club in Phnom Penh called the Heart of Darkness (ominously named after the Joseph Conrad novel that inspired the film *Apocalypse Now*). Eddie was obviously keen on her because he went back to see her on his second visit. Ami and Eddie hung out together, she stayed in his room at different hotels, he visited the small wooden shack where she lived with her parents and they seemed to have had a sweet relationship.

Over these couple of weeks, Ami's father died and, because she had no money, Eddie paid for the funeral. There was even a video of the funeral, which Jo eventually got hold of. 'For me, finding Ami was the biggest breakthrough,' she says. 'Eddie is on that video and he doesn't look like he's on drugs or anything. He looks like Eddie. He has his arms round Ami from time to time and they look as though they were close. Eddie was obviously trying to help her out. At her father's wake, they look very happy together.'

Not long afterwards, Mike went back to Cambodia with Eddie's godfather. They met up with Ami and asked her questions about what Eddie had done during that time. She confirmed that she had been with him until 24 October. The other significant person was a young man called Trip. Eddie had befriended him on his first visit. 'Trip hangs around the border next to Thailand,' says Jo, 'and he organised for Eddie and his friends to go to Angkor Wat, which is when they became friends. Trip is one of the individuals Eddie had talked about when he came back to England. Mike even eventually got the police to interview him, but he did not have any information.'

Meanwhile, Ami told them that Eddie had said he was going to Thailand with two friends after he left her on 24 October. He promised her that he would come back to see her in three weeks time. Ami also told Eddie's father that they had been thinking of living together and even having babies. 'He would say that,' says Jo, 'because he didn't want to be unkind. He had a string of different women around the world, so I don't take that too seriously.' The wooden shack where she lived had not had any improvements made to it. Ami wasn't living the high life. Of course, during this time, the possibility that Eddie had been murdered remained.

In November 2005, Mike went out again and this time met

the Prime Minister of Cambodia. Jo and he had the idea that the best course of action would be to get some British detectives out there to do an investigation. They were disillusioned with the Cambodian police and thought the British would do a better job, but Cambodian protocol dictated that they had to have a Prime Ministerial invitation. They were successful. 'Mike also met up with a private detective from Australia who said he could help us,' she says. 'We ended up taking him on and he's been on the case now for two years. But he hasn't come up with anything useful and we have paid him a lot of money.'

Neither Mike nor Jo went out to Cambodia in 2006. They left the enquiries to the private detective. And finally in the June of that year, a team of British detectives did go out to look for Eddie. 'This was great news for us,' she says. 'We had to work so hard to enable it to actually take place. In fact, it was the first time ever that British police had been allowed in the country. That felt like a major coup.'

The British detectives were there for two weeks and Mike and Jo were sure they would find out what had happened. 'They were a crime investigation unit,' she says, 'so they knew what they were doing and they did interview a lot of people.

'But in the end, frustratingly, they concluded that they didn't know what had happened and they didn't come up with any new information.'

Jo was disappointed but decided to take no news as good news. Maybe Eddie's still there, she thought to herself, and too scared to come home. Even as a small child, Eddie had been adventurous. He was in and out of cupboards at home.

'That was the beginning of his personality,' says Jo. 'He also always used to make people laugh. Eddie was always the centre of attention without quite meaning to be.' As Eddie grew up, he was also fearless. He was always willing to take risks. At school, he was a character, intelligent but often in trouble. 'Like when he was a teenager, he went on a school trip to France and the teachers couldn't find him or his friend. He was eventually found in the girls' changing room. Not that the girls minded. He was a mischievous boy but everyone loved him.'

However, Eddie went on to get ten GCSEs, mostly As and Bs, then three As at A-level in Business Studies, IT and Communication Studies. 'He worked really hard for them,' says Jo. 'All his friends would be on the beach but he'd shut himself in his room so he deserved his results. When he wanted to be, he was utterly focused. In this case, he wanted to beat Elliott's results. Elliott got two Bs and a C, so Eddie had to do better. He was competitive with himself. He was very happy to have succeeded but he didn't brag; that wasn't his style.'

His gap year was a huge success. Eight of them, girls and boys, all old school friends, went off travelling together. Eddie was always a bit of a wheeler and dealer so he made money for his trip by selling whatever he could on eBay. He'd go to car boot sales, he'd buy his friends' unwanted possessions and he'd make money from them. When Eddie wanted to do something, he would make sure it actually happened.

One of Jo's favourite memories is of joining Eddie in Australia earlier in 2004. 'He was there as part of his gap year and it was his birthday. He was 19 so Tony and I went over to visit him there, ' she explains. 'Mike and Max had already been. Eddie had bought a Cadillac while he was there and they'd travelled up the east coast to Cairns and stayed quite a few weeks in Surfer's Paradise on the way. He loved Australia but he was really looking forward to some real travelling in the Far East.'

In fact, Jo had some of the happiest days of her life with him there. 'I took Eddie to the hairdressers. He wanted a few blond highlights put in. He was so handsome and charming, and all the stylists clustered around him. I felt immensely proud,' she says. Afterwards, they lunched beside Sydney Opera House and talked and talked. 'He was my son but he was also my friend,' she says movingly. 'He held my hand in his enormous hands. It was so sweet.'

Jo also took him to hospital because he'd broken his wrist up on the Gold Coast and it needed more attention. 'Eddie told me that he'd broken his wrist playing football on the beach,' she says. 'But five months after he'd gone missing, I found out from his friends that he'd actually fallen twenty-five feet from an apartment onto the beach. They were having a party and the balcony was very low, which explains why the break was so bad. I'm sure Ed didn't tell me these details because he didn't want me to worry.'

After that, he and his friends went off to Bangkok, Laos, Burma, Vietnam and Cambodia. As his family was to discover, it was Cambodia that really affected him. 'The people there have nothing,' he would say when he got back, 'but they are happier than us with everything.' It was an attraction that cost him and his family very, very dearly.

In January 2007, Jo and Mike went back to Cambodia once again. 'We'd just had another Christmas without Eddie, 'she says, 'and I really felt it would be good to get on TV and radio out there again and appeal to everyone as a mother who was being tormented by the disappearance of her son. I wanted to implore anyone who knows anything to come forward. I want to stop living in limbo and discover what happened to Eddie. Even if he's dead, it's better than living like this.'

His parents offered US $20,000 for information. 'We decided to put a figure on the money,' she says, 'so it's more real to people. That's a lot of money in a country where the average policeman earns just US $300 a year. We desperately hope it will tempt people to tell the truth. Someone must know something.'

Jo's biggest fear is that someone killed Eddie for his money. He had £3,000 when he left the UK, but what did he do with it? Jo really wants to establish how he was carrying his money and if he had traveller's cheques or had opened a bank account out there. This information will help them form an opinion at least about whether Eddie was simply murdered for his cash.

'I don't know how discreet he was with it. He was always very careful with money,' she says, 'but life is cheap in Cambodia and, as a result of so much violence and death in their culture, people are hardened to killing.'

At the moment, Jo and Mike cannot move forward. They still do not know what happened to their son. It seemed that he was planning to leave Cambodia and go to Thailand, perhaps to catch his flight home. However, there is no evidence that he ever left Cambodia. They've been up to the border between Thailand and Cambodia and seen how lawless it is. But they still don't know if Eddie made it there.

Jo keeps his room at home unchanged. It's full of souvenirs from his trips. She treasures them for his sake and reads his diaries to keep herself feeling close to him. They have great support from friends and family. His brothers raise money by doing sponsored runs and providing the cash to fund the private detective. Everyone is doing their bit. But all of this doesn't alter the unpalatable reality. They still don't know what has happened to Eddie. 'Sometimes, I look at the email from him that says he's going to clear his head and decide what he's going to do for the next three years, ' she says, 'and wonder whether he will just walk back in the door this October.'

In the meantime, Jo, Mike and their family are not giving up. They're intending to go back to Cambodia again this year and put more pressure on the Cambodian police. There are more questions to be asked. The police haven't spoken to the passengers who sat next to Eddie on the way out there – did he say anything to them? Jo is not about to stop searching. And she never will.

Chapter Three

I Just Want My Husband to Come Home

Boyish-looking 33-year-old Mark Roberts and his wife, 42-year-old Sharon, have always been deeply in love. Nine years ago, when they got married at a wonderful service in Canterbury, neither Mark nor Sharon could possibly have envisaged circumstances that would lead to Mark leaving their home and disappearing. Such an eventuality just didn't exist on their love map. They were a devoted couple.

However, on 15 May 2006, Mark walked out of their flat in Whitstable, Kent, and Sharon hasn't seen him since that fateful day.

Sharon – a pretty redhead who works for Laura Ashley – was brought up as part of a big family in Canterbury. 'I'm the eldest. I've got four brothers and two sisters.' She smiles. 'I loved my childhood; it was all about the family. I couldn't have asked for better parents. Dad, who had been a long-distance lorry driver, died in 1992 but my mum's still going strong and I see a lot of her. Two of my brothers are in the army now but I see my nieces and nephews. We're a close family. I had wonderful parents. I couldn't have had a better upbringing.'

The same cannot be said for Mark and his family. He did not have a very happy family life. He has one brother, Tony, a half-brother, David and a sister, Rosie, and when he was seven, he and his sister were sent into care. Mark ended up at a children's home, while Rosie was taken in by foster parents. It was obviously a harsh upbringing for Mark, one where affection and cuddles were in short supply. The children's home in South Wales where he ended up is the one where years later a network of abuse was uncovered. Sharon has no idea if Mark was sexually abused at this home but it was a possibility. 'He wouldn't talk about it,' she says. He preferred to remain silent on the subject, possibly because it was such an emotionally loaded area of his life.

When Mark was 11, he was sent to live with foster parents in Stevenage. Apparently, he was happy there and even had a good time at school, where he actually enjoyed learning for the first time. Mark went into the junior section of the army when he was 14 and into the adult army at 16. He explained later to Sharon that it was his way of escaping everything he'd had to put up with so far. He was giving himself a life. 'He also said he learned a lot about discipline and how to look after himself. He was very good at ironing and cooking and that was thanks to the army,' she says. 'In fact, I think that training will help him survive now that he's disappeared.'

Mark was only 17 when he did his first tour of Northern Ireland. That meant he was too young to walk around on the streets there, at least at first. He remembered children spitting at him and also was traumatised by seeing one of his commanding officers having his head blown off. 'It deeply affected him, but again he didn't like to talk about it,' she says. 'That's just the sort of man he is. But I don't think holding on to all those feelings did him any good. He loved the travelling in the army and the outdoor aspects of that life but he saw some terrible things and I can't help thinking they affected him for the rest of his life. '

However, Mark bought himself out of the army when he was 22. 'He said he'd seen too much,' explains Sharon. 'I knew he'd lost another friend in Germany, playing chicken on the autobahn. They were drunk. His friend wouldn't return to the barracks. Mark tried to persuade him but he ended up leaving him. His friend went too far – he lost his life on what should have been a jolly night out with the lads. Again, Mark was badly affected. He felt guilty. He felt he could have done something else to save his friend. He even went AWOL and ended up in the army prison at Chichester. Recently, I discovered that Mark tried to commit suicide after his friend died. He even tried to go to the funeral but they wouldn't let him in. I think he got more and more rebellious after that. So it wasn't surprising that he was keen to get out.'

Mark and Sharon met in 1995. By this time, Mark had found work as a security guard at British Home Stores in Canterbury, which is where Sharon was employed in the knitwear department. Mark was 22, with dark hair and lovely brown eyes, while Sharon was pretty, petite, 31 and divorced. She had already had a violent relationship with her first husband, David.

'I worked at McDonald's for a while to earn some extra cash when I left school. David was older than me by a couple of years and he worked there,' she explains. 'I was very inexperienced with men and I thought we were in love. But he was a diabetic and, after we were married, he started to suffer from terrible mood swings. I was too young to know what I was letting myself in for. As soon as I realised, I left him.'

That experience of marriage put Sharon off relationships for the next five years. 'I got into jazz dance, tap, then baton twirling instead. I stayed away from men,' she says. When Mark started working at BHS, she was still not interested in men. 'He noticed me; that's how it happened,' she says proudly. 'I was friends with one of the plain-clothed detectives there and she asked me one day if I knew that the good-looking security guard was spending rather a lot of time watching me on the CCTV screen. I was surprised and pleased.'

Sharon hadn't realised or really taken any notice of this boyish-looking security guard, but she did after that. There was one occasion in the staff room when Sharon and Mark happened to be both getting coffee at the same time and they just started chatting spontaneously. Almost immediately, they discovered that they both loved Wales. 'Mark had trained with the army up near Snowdonia,' she says. 'My dad loved Wales and we'd scattered his ashes up there at Swallow Falls. This was our common bond. It would continue to be a bond throughout our relationship.'

Mark had a persuasive effect on Sharon. 'He was so easy to talk to,' she says. 'He was the first man for years to make me feel relaxed. He was also very attractive and his eyes were very soft. I noticed his eyes straightaway. They gave away something sensitive about his character – I fell for his eyes.'

Then one evening after work, Sharon's friend let her down. Sharon had been going to go to the cinema with her. 'Mark immediately asked if he could come instead.' She laughs. 'It was to see *Cold Mountain*. He made me laugh a lot. That was really the first time since my dad died in 1992 that I'd relaxed in that way. I realised I was enjoying myself. Mark walked me home and then he asked if we were going out or not?'

Sharon's response was immediate. 'Do you know how old I am?' she asked, thinking he wouldn't realise that she was nine years older than him. But Mark knew because he'd been doing his research on her. 'That nine years older never made any difference to our relationship,' she says. 'It didn't matter. It never mattered. He simply said, "I like you, I get on with you."' After that, they lived in each other's pockets. They were falling in love. Mark would take her to Paris for the weekend, or bring her roses. He was open, honest, flattering and affectionate. How could she not fall for him?

Having left the army recently, Mark didn't have anywhere to live. His mother lived in a mobile home just outside Canterbury, but that wasn't really suitable for him. He ended up spending more and more time at Sharon's house. 'My mum could see how happy he made me,' she says, 'and she knew how long I'd been on my own. So she'd have him round for dinner and let him sleep on the sofa. In the end, she suggested that Mark and I have one of the double bedrooms in the house. It was very kind of her. It was a bit strange for me because Mark and I hadn't been sleeping together until that point. But it was also great to have him in my home.'

For Mark, this newfound family life was a novelty. He'd never really had a close family around him and he loved their cosiness with each other. It felt like the loving environment that he'd missed out on as a child and teenager. However, he also found it difficult because he'd never had this kind of family experience before and he couldn't understand how it worked. 'He hadn't spoken to his brothers and sister for years,' says Sharon. 'They'd never learned how to communicate properly or build up a proper relationship. My mum always said his mum wasn't a maternal mother. Our family represented something completely new and he felt very welcomed into it, but he found some of the communication difficult. But we embraced him into our family.'

Sometimes it was hard for Mark. For instance, he really didn't want to be met by questions about his day. It felt intrusive to him. Additionally, he didn't get it at all at Christmas, when they gave each other really lovely presents that they actually wanted. 'I used to just get socks and sweets,' he would say, not understanding what it meant to give presents to the ones you love. That seemed alien to him.

After a year of seeing each other, Mark started to ask Sharon if she would think about marrying him. At first, she rebuffed him. The last thing she wanted was another failed marriage. But he persevered and, finally, a friend of Sharon's had a word with her. 'I realised that Mark wasn't like David, my first husband,' she says, 'and we were having a very loving, intense relationship. We were even talking about moving to Wales together. I felt safe with him. He was very romantic and he was always looking after me. One weekend, we went to Rye together and it was very special. We stayed at the ancient smuggler's pub, the Mermaid Inn. Mark asked me to marry him again and this time I said "Yes". Again we talked about moving to Wales together. The atmosphere was beautiful and I knew he was the right man for me. We got engaged on Christmas Eve 1997.'

The wedding was on 20 June 1998, in Canterbury. Mark had been working overseas doing security work, while Sharon painstakingly planned all the wedding arrangements. They got married in a registry office, then had a blessing at a local church. 'I had a champagne-satin wedding gown, which was like saloon-girl dress,' she says enthusiastically. 'It had a tight bodice and a bustle. Mark wore a blue-grey morning suit and it was a fantastic day. We spent our honeymoon in Wales, near Swallow Falls. It was perfect. We also had a few days at the Disneyland near Paris because I'm a big kid really and Mark never had that sort of childhood, so he loved it too.'

They even started talking about having children. The newlyweds continued to live with Sharon's mother because they were saving to be able to afford to move to Wales. 'Mark got work as a security guard but the jobs were never stable so he could never depend on getting that money,' she explains. 'It made it difficult to save, so my mum offered us a room for a bit longer.'

Mark had an idea. He was tired of working as a security guard and wanted to establish something more permanent. He decided to set up a shop selling new-age products, so that he could be at home more and so he could establish himself financially before they moved to Wales. That was the plan anyway. 'Mark had always had this gentle, spiritual side,' she says. 'He read angel cards and was psychic. He wanted to set up a shop selling candles, books and quirky gifts. The trouble was, he also wanted to run before he could walk. He wasn't very practical about it.'

He had his first shop down the road in Herne Bay but that didn't work because the location wasn't right. Mark found a couple of investors and moved to premises in Whitstable. 'This was 2002. We moved to a little flat in Whitstable and Mark tried to get his business going. The eventual aim was always moving to Wales but it was never to be. It was as if the universe conspired against us,' she says.

Mark studied the healing-energy therapy reiki and was interested in feng shui. He enjoyed this new direction in his life and spending time making friends with his customers. In fact, his shop was just starting to go well when disaster hit. His investors went bankrupt and dragged him down with them.

'He was devastated,' says Sharon. 'All his dreams were destroyed. He didn't tell me for a while but the bailiffs came and seized his stock. His shop couldn't survive. Its closure was a huge blow for Mark and I don't think he ever got over it. He'd been trying hard to give us some financial security and provide a way to move to Wales, but now this all seemed impossible. He felt as though he'd failed me and failed himself too.'

Mark's self-confidence took a fatal blow. At first, his bank was happy to let him take his time to pay off his debt but then it changed its mind. Mark became terribly anxious about his finances and concerned that he was being a hopeless husband. 'This is when he said to me, "You could do better than me," for the first time,' says Sharon, 'and I just couldn't convince him that I was content with him however he was and whatever was happening to him. However hard I tried, he didn't believe me. In fact, I didn't care about money; I cared that we were together. Mark was always such a loving, romantic husband. He'd always make an effort for me, like buying me flowers or tickets to the cinema. He was a fantastically caring man and I loved him, but I didn't seem to be getting through to him.'

Little things started happening, which indicated just how low he was feeling. Instead of going out in the evening with Sharon, he'd encourage her to go out with her mother. 'He felt he didn't deserve an evening out and he didn't want me to have to pay for him,' she explains. 'His self-esteem was plummeting. Any remaining self-belief was disappearing rapidly.'

Something had to change and Mark knew it. Eventually, he spotted an advert for a security job on a building site in Wales, so he went off for the interview. 'He didn't want to do security work again but he saw it as a necessity,' she says. 'He thought if he based himself in Wales, it would be another way of us getting there. He got the job and they needed him straightaway. So he stayed there. He ended up living in a caravan on the site. The idea was that he'd save some money in order to rent a house for us and I'd get a transfer to a Laura Ashley shop up there. To be honest, I was pleased because I thought that at least this was a step forward again, although I was also a bit worried about him being on his own and how he would cope. I thought he might get very lonely. But I tried to look at this new job in a positive way.'

It was July 2005 and, because of the bankruptcy, Mark was already emotionally, physically and mentally run down when he started the job. Sharon and Mark were in daily contact and, fortunately, had planned a few days away in Ashdown Forest near Tunbridge Wells to celebrate Mark's 33rd birthday before he got this work. 'We went off to Winnie the Pooh country,' she says. 'We always had a thing about bears between us. It was our way of saying that we loved each other. We gave each other bears as presents. We were really happy during these days. We were so excited to see one another. I thought he was in really good spirits and hoped that meant he was picking up in general. I noticed he slept a lot. I don't think he was getting much sleep in that caravan. It must have been very noisy. But at this point, I wasn't worried about him.'

Afterwards, they were in regular phone contact again but the following week, Mark said something strange to her. 'He said, "I'm really sorry that I treated you like this and I'll make it up to you," she recalls. 'I didn't know what he was talking about.'

On 25 September, Sharon went up to Wales to see Mark on her way to see her brother and his children in the Midlands. Sharon's mother had had an unnerving phone call from Mark. He had told her that he didn't want Sharon to go up to Llandudno because the Freemasons were chasing him and they would chase her as well. Obviously, his grasp on reality was going and he appeared to be having paranoid delusions. 'I got on a coach and went to see him and it was dreadful,' she says. 'The Mark I met was nothing like my Mark. He was dishevelled and disorientated. He thought I'd been there for three hours already and he'd been searching for me in local hotels. He thought there were people stopping him finding me. And he told me to go home because these people would get me as well.'

The local police told Sharon that Mark had had a rough night and they'd found him wandering in the road. Sharon had no idea what to do. They suggested that she should take him to a doctor as soon as possible. Meanwhile, Mark was claiming that his drink had been spiked and that was the reason for his loss of mental clarity. Sharon phoned the doctor but she was told that they wouldn't be able to check Mark's blood for drugs because too much time had elapsed and that Mark sounded as though he was exhausted. It was obvious to everyone that the best place for him was home.

Mark agreed to go home with her to Whitstable. Sharon thought he'd get some good rest and recover. He'd been doing difficult shifts on the construction site in Llandudno which had made sleeping difficult, but she had no idea how far his mental health had gone downhill. 'I wanted him to come home and feel looked after,' she says. 'I hoped that he'd settle down when he was with me again.' But that wasn't what happened.

Mark sat in their flat becoming more and more withdrawn. 'He could hear people shouting at him,' says Sharon, 'and it was really terrible when it got to a stage where he wouldn't eat my dinners. He thought I'd put poison in his food. That was really hard for me because I loved him and food was one of the ways I cared for him, but now he wouldn't let me. I felt very hurt when this was going on. I didn't really understand that this was part of him having a mental breakdown.'

Sharon tried her best to get him to see a doctor but Mark absolutely refused. It was obvious that he was going through some sort of illness, but trying to get help for him proved impossible. Sharon discovered that doctors cannot come out to a patient unless the patient gives permission. She was in a Catch-22 situation: Mark wouldn't see a doctor and the doctor wouldn't come if he didn't ask him to. A long-term result of Mark's case was that Sharon became involved in campaigning for the law to be changed but, at the time, the only option was for her to have Mark sectioned. She couldn't bear to go down that harsh route.

Consequently, Mark stayed at home, getting worse and worse. He would leave taps running in the house, convinced that he was accessing fresher water. He'd go into rages against his own demons, though never against Sharon, and at other times he'd cry like a baby. 'He'd also say again and again that he'd let me down,' she says. 'He was obviously in a lot of pain and I often felt helpless around it. I just tried to be there for him anyway.'

Obviously, Mark couldn't go back to Wales. He wasn't well enough. Sharon wondered whether something had happened to him there. 'He'd say, "You don't want to know what I saw," but I didn't know whether he was talking about something that happened in Wales or whether he was talking about being in the army, or whether he was going back to his childhood in care,' she says. Living with such high levels of anxiety around Mark started to take its toll on Sharon's own health. She was trying on a bridesmaid's dress for a relative's wedding when she mentioned to her mother that she had lots of pain in her back, which turned out to be shingles.

Mark's mental turmoil was increasing and Sharon felt as though he didn't trust her now. She'd become an enemy along with the rest of the world. A disturbing turning point for Sharon, by now the breadwinner for the couple, was when she discovered that Mark had gone to the bank and taken out her tax-credit money. 'He'd had to take my passport to do it and I was horrified,' she says. 'That was a step too far. I decided to call in the police. I thought they might help him.'

Sharon felt totally alone with Mark and his illness, so she thought the police might be able to see that something was wrong with Mark and do something. Quite honestly, she needed support and didn't know where to get it. However, the police interviewed him and he was able to answer the questions cogently, hiding his deteriorating mental state. Mark even accused Sharon of being the one having the problems. The police couldn't help unless he was self-harming, or attacking other people. Sharon felt powerless and in despair.

In the meantime, their marriage was severely challenged. They loved one another but trust was breaking down. Mark felt as though he was a failure. Sharon wasn't getting any support and was very anxious. She had no idea what to do. They were both desperate. One day in March, Mark took off and didn't come back. 'He left me a letter, which was saying goodbye, and I thought he'd really gone for good, but he rang me from France and asked if I wanted him to come home. Of course, I did,' says Sharon. On that occasion, he was only missing for a couple of days. They both thought a bit of space apart from one another might sort them out. It didn't. The anguish continued.

Mark spent the whole of 15 May 2006 repeatedly saying he was going to leave. Sharon begged him not to go. 'But I couldn't get through to him,' she says. 'He kept saying that he was really sorry that he couldn't give me what I needed and deserved, that he couldn't give me security.' Sharon wasn't sure whether to stay at home or go to work. She'd already taken a lot of time off, so they hugged and kissed as usual and she went for the bus to Laura Ashley.

When she got home he really had gone. 'In the back of my mind, I was thinking he'd go off for a few days and then come back,' she says, 'but he didn't. I took it as a good sign that he hadn't taken many clothes, but that turned out to be irrelevant.'

This time, Mark had taken his wedding ring off and left it behind. This action contained a symbolic message – their marriage, he seemed to be saying, was over. 'I thought this meant he didn't love me any more,' says Sharon, 'but I also remembered that I'd taken off my wedding rings before he left and I deeply regretted that afterwards. I understood that, in fact, he'd got the message from me that our marriage was over. I have to admit there was also a part of me that thought it might be good for him to spend some time on his own getting his head sorted out. A part of me accepted I might have to sit back and let him get on with it for a while.'

However, Sharon was thinking that two weeks would be enough time for him to confront what was happening in his head. 'But after two weeks, I'd heard nothing and I was walking round like a zombie,' she says. 'I was waiting for the phone to ring and it never did. I wasn't sleeping either. I was also worried because he'd hardly taken any clothes with him and I knew he hadn't been thinking rationally when he left, because he didn't take his mobile charger either.'

Sharon has a rabbit that is allowed into the house and roams around freely. Mark knows how special this rabbit is to Sharon. But he didn't phone on the rabbit's birthday. Then there was their wedding anniversary in June. 'I knew I wasn't going to get a card from him,' she says. 'I knew he thought our marriage was over.' Sharon thought he might have gone back to Wales but she called the construction site and he wasn't there. Finally, after a month, she reported him missing to the police and then the charity Missing People.

The police came round and took photos of him and bank statements away with them. Sharon couldn't find their wedding album and she still can't. She wonders if Mark had taken it. Maybe he wanted to keep it with him to remind himself of just how good they were together. 'On our sixth anniversary, he'd suggested that we renew our wedding vows in a tiny church in Wales,' she explains. 'So we did. It was just us, our mothers and four friends. Mark's eyes welled up as he whispered to me, "I don't deserve you." We had had such a strong marriage. I still couldn't believe it was in tatters.'

Mark's medical records from the army were called in by the police. This was how Sharon discovered that he had tried to commit suicide when he was in the military prison in Chichester. 'I was looking for answers to what had happened,' she says. 'And that friend of his had died playing chicken on the motorway in Germany, plus his commanding officer who had been blown up in Ireland. He'd seen some terrible things and I wondered if they had come to haunt him at this later stage. I wondered if they'd caused his mental breakdown. I wondered if he was suffering from post-traumatic stress disorder.'

Sharon heard nothing until 12 December 2006, when a letter arrived at her flat. It was addressed to Mark so she knew it wasn't from him. It was from a hospital in France where he'd been treated for a couple of days with a heart complaint. 'He'd had a problem with his heart since childhood,' she says, 'so he must have had to go and get it checked out. I was excited for a short while, because at least I knew he was alive and working in France. I guessed he was working in vineyards there because I knew he loved them. The police tried to get more information about who took him there but they didn't find out anything useful. In the end, I felt helpless yet again.'

Sharon spent Christmas 2006 with her family but she sat by the phone just in case Mark rang. 'It was terrible,' she says. 'I'd never have got through it on my own. It felt really wrong without Mark. I needed to feel he was still with me. I wrote a card to him and put it with a little bear under my tree – the tree that normally Mark would decorate – just in case he came home for Christmas while I was staying at my mum's. He hadn't had any soft toys when he was young at the Dr Barnados home, so Mark and I had decided over the years that we would make up for that. But it was a gloomy Christmas for me, despite my family around me. Mark didn't get in contact.'

There was no word from him at New Year either. Now Sharon was really worrying about Mark again. 'I started to think something awful might have happened to him,' she says, 'but then another envelope arrived. This time it was from a German police station and again it was addressed to Mark. It contained a letter which showed that Mark had been into that police station and reported that a cross and chain had gone missing. Suddenly, I felt a glimmer of hope again, because at least I knew he was alive. Although I was frustrated that the German police hadn't picked up on him being a missing person through their computer files.'

Mark had always been an inveterate romantic and celebrated Valentine's Day with Sharon in all sorts of imaginative ways, so she was hopeful again on 14 February. 'He was such a loving man that he'd leave a trail of rose petals that led up to a hot bath with candles,' she says. 'Then he'd have cooked a meal for us. That's the sort of husband he was. He'd always buy me a single red rose.' But not this Valentine's Day. Again she heard nothing.

However, on her 43rd birthday on 8 March 2007, something momentous, hopeful and simply amazing happened to Sharon. 'I'd been out with family for the day,' she says, 'but when I got home there was an envelope with a German stamp on the mat. I knew that Mark had sent me something. I opened it cautiously because I was dreading that he'd written saying our marriage was over.' Then came the floods of tears. And the relief. 'It was a spiritual card,' she says. 'It had lots of glittery angels on it. It didn't say "Happy birthday, wife." But it did say, "Hope you are well and have a wonderful birthday. Enjoy your year. Love Mark xxx." It also had a PS. And the PS was extremely significant. It said, "Will always think of you and us.""

Sharon's heart almost burst with joy. She couldn't believe that, after the long silences, Mark was actually getting in contact. On 10 April, she got a call from Mark telling her he was in Germany, working in a restaurant, and that he'd like her to go out there to visit him. She talked to him on the telephone a few times over the next few months, hoping naturally that they would get together soon. But it gradually became apparent that Mark was still a little confused, then he disappeared out of contact again in August. They had arranged that Sharon would go out to Munich in early September – Mark's birthday is on the 4th – and that he would meet her there. Sadly, Sharon went but Mark didn't turn up. Gradually, Sharon has had to stop thinking about Mark and start thinking about her own health. No longer so hopeful that there will be a reunion with Mark, she intends to move to Wales on her own as a way of symbolising that she has moved on. She is still campaigning to change the law with regard to relatives being able to get medical help for their loved ones who are suffering mental health problems, as opposed to sectioning them. Sharon is a courageous woman who deserves her own happy ending.

Chapter Four

Why Hasn't Anyone Found My Mum?

Tyler Blake is a tall, dark-haired, eight-year-old boy who lives in Frindsbury, near Rochester in Kent. Tragically, he hasn't seen his mum, Rebecca, since she disappeared on 25 November 2002, when he was three. Of course, he can't really understand what has happened because nobody can tell him – they just don't know. Tall, slim, blonde, attractive 22-year-old Rebecca Carr went missing that afternoon and there haven't been any positive sightings of her since. Her lovely son simply wants to know why nobody has found his mum yet.

'There is no closure when someone goes missing,' says Rebecca's mother, Lynne. 'The not knowing is agonising and for a child it must be ten times worse. Tyler cannot understand what has happened to his mum and he desperately wants to know. It has been awful to see him in turmoil, although he's actually a lot calmer at the moment.'

Lynne, who looks like an older version of her daughter, gave birth to Rebecca when she was 21. 'I was still living with my mum and dad. I was with her father, Bill, for nearly three years and we did briefly live together,' she says, 'but Mum and Dad really helped me out with her as a baby. Mum and Dad were only in their forties, plus my two brothers were still living at home and everyone doted on Rebecca. She was very spoilt.'

Primary school went well for Rebecca. Lynne was working as a van driver delivering car parts so her parents often looked after Rebecca. 'She was doing brilliantly,' says Lynne, 'but when I had my second daughter, Laura, and she was seven, she was a bit put out. Rebecca had always had all the attention and now she had a baby sister that had come along and was getting all that adoring attention instead. Looking back, I think that could have affected her.'

Rebecca was getting more and more troubled. 'She started to get difficult,' says Lynne. 'I got married to a new husband, not her father, when she was four, so that was probably another reason why she felt fed up and angry. By this time, we'd got our own place but Rebecca kept running away to her nan and granddad's down the road. I expect she missed being with them because we were all very close. She was making a protest. Sometimes, I think now if it'd been just me and her, it would have been OK but you can't think like that, can you?'

Rebecca didn't like secondary school. She was outspoken and rebellious; she wanted to do her own thing. Her mother didn't know what to do with her. 'She was rude to teachers,' says Lynne. 'In her teens, she'd run away from school. She had bad luck too though. Every time she messed up, somehow she always got caught. They went on a camping trip and Rebecca was caught smoking in her tent. A group of them climbed up onto the swimming pool roof – she got caught. I tried to talk to her about it but she never took any notice. She was strong minded; she would do what she wanted to do.'

Horse-riding was Rebecca's passion and escape. 'She loved horses,' says Lynne. 'She went to some stables nearby every weekend and that's where she really enjoyed herself. We even borrowed a horse for her, for a while. She was so happy when she was with her horses. I love remembering that.'

She was physically head and shoulders above her friends at school, which did make her in some ways the odd one out. With no interest in academic subjects, Rebecca decided to leave school at 16. At least she loved horses so she went to work at the stables. 'It was fantastic. She was working towards getting all her certificates to become a horse-riding instructor and she was doing very well. She was in her glory at those stables,' says Lynne, 'but then she found a boyfriend called Gary. I hate to say this, but her attention was then distracted away from her beloved horses. She'd never had a proper boyfriend before and by the time she was eighteen she was pregnant.'

At first, Lynne admits she was disappointed but, soon afterwards, she and the rest of the family all became enthusiastic about the idea of having a new baby in their midst. 'I knew Rebecca would make a very good mother,' says Lynne, 'and she was over the moon. She gave birth to Tyler in the same hospital as she was born in and we were all very excited.'

By this time, the council had given Rebecca, Gary and Tyler a flat in Rochester so they weren't far away. 'We went over beforehand and decorated Tyler's room,' says Rebecca's sister, Laura, now 20. 'We really enjoyed preparing the room for him. I was over there all the time helping out. Especially when Tyler had been born. It was bliss. I loved it that my older sister was a mother. She'd been my big sister but she'd looked after me a lot – now I had the opportunity to look after her baby. I used to love having Tyler home with us. He'd even sleep in his carrycot in my room. It was a special time, although I wasn't seeing so much of Rebecca in those days. But we were all very close.'

Sadly, the bubble of new babydom didn't last. 'They had money problems because Gary was often out of work and they ended up getting evicted,' explains Lynne. That's when they started living in lots of different sorts of accommodation. It was a very unsettled existence and I helped them out as much as I could. But in the end, they needed more than I could give them.'

Tyler started staying at his grandma's house a lot. 'Rebecca was a dedicated mother,' says Lynne. 'But Gary and her fell on hard times and they didn't seem to be able to pick themselves up. They had lots of different bedsits and hotel accommodation so it was very hard to bring up Tyler living like that. She used to come and stay with me for a few days at a time. Laura was also a massive help. But Rebecca would never leave it more that a couple of days before she would turn up for him.' It was a very difficult time for Rebecca. A series of shabby bedsits and no money coming in made life unstable and uncomfortable for her.

On 23 November 2002, Rebecca and Gary called round to pick up three-year-old Tyler from his grandma. They were in a vibrant mood, happy to take their chatty little boy off for the day. However, little did Lynne realise that their worlds were just about to break into tiny, irretrievable pieces.

Horrifically, that was the last time Lynne saw her blonde, beautiful daughter. Two days later, Rebecca disappeared without trace. And Tyler, poor little Tyler, has lost his mum.

'My parents were the last ones to see her,' says Lynne. 'On Monday, 25 November, Rebecca called them and asked if they would give her a lift from Chatham to Gillingham. Tyler stayed with Gary. They went and got her, dropped her in Gillingham and no one has seen her since.' The facts are so simple but the effect has been devastating.

In fact, it took some time for her family to realise Rebecca was really missing because they were used to her disappearing into the undergrowth of poverty. But this was different. Her sister, Laura, had last seen her a couple of weeks earlier. 'She was at the house and we chatted. Typically, she'd bought me a new jumper. That was really sweet of her. Because I didn't see her much at that point, it took me weeks to realise that she had actually gone,' says Laura.

For a while, Lynne wasn't worried either. She was used to Rebecca being out of contact for a few days. 'After a week, I reported her missing to the police. But I still expected her to show up at any time,' she says. 'I couldn't imagine that she would be able to go very long without seeing her little boy. After all, Rebecca loves being a mum to Tyler. The police were very good. They told the charity Missing People and the local radio station, and they did a report on her. But it was, and still is, as though Rebecca simply disappeared off the face of the earth that afternoon. No one has reported seeing her.'

There is no convenient explanation for how or why Rebecca went missing. Certainly, her close family have no idea what caused it. There is no indication that she had any intention of walking out of her life. She loved her little son too much. Naturally, Tyler is the one who is the most affected by her disappearance. He is a little boy who just does not understand where his mum is or why she isn't with him. It has been terrible for him in every single way, especially psychologically and emotionally.

'His father, Gary and I looked after him at first,' says Lynne. 'I was happy to look after my grandson until this situation had been sorted out. But it ended up being Laura and I who took most of the responsibility for looking after Tyler as time went by. I love my grandson so much, but I was going through such a terrible time myself over Rebecca that it became hard to cope, even with Laura helping. The trouble was I was going through a horrendous depression. I wouldn't answer the door. I wouldn't answer the telephone. I was in a terrible state. Fortunately, Laura was my rock. She was always there for me, encouraging me to get on with my life. But it wasn't good for Tyler to be around me all the time because I couldn't be totally there for him and he was having his own problems. Poor Tyler – it was so awful for him.'

Lynne looked after Tyler for a year but she was so distressed it was decided that it would be better for him if he went to live with foster parents. So at five, Tyler was allocated his first set of foster parents. 'This was a dreadful time,' says Lynne. 'Social services wanted him to be adopted, but that way we wouldn't see him. I wanted him to be fostered so that the family could all stay in close contact with him. But the first set of foster parents didn't work out. Tyler was having therapy sessions but he was very angry and he kept running away from them. He had terrible psychological problems around his missing mummy and, in the end, that relationship broke up. He was very unsettled and we were all very worried.'

Little Tyler has had to grow up before his time. He's had to face a dark side of reality at such a young age. Not surprisingly, his mum's unexplained disappearance has had an enormous effect on him. 'Of course, he couldn't have an adult perspective. At least we can see that the police, the papers and the Missing People charity have done as much as they can to look for Rebecca,' says Lynne. 'But to Tyler, he can't understand why no one has found his mum. He felt angry with everyone for not finding her. He was also blaming himself. He thought that his mum left because of him. He has his own sad little story about when she disappeared. It's about his mum going to the shop and Gary and him waiting for his mum to come back. And she never did. That's his little story and it's heart rending.'

Over time, Lynne began to accept, however hard it was, that Rebecca was missing. 'At first, you're on the edge of your seat all the time,' says Lynne, 'but gradually you come to terms with the fact that she's gone and there's nothing you can do. I write on a calendar every day and keep a diary of my thoughts – that helps as well.'

On one occasion, a girl of Rebecca's age was found on the local railway lines and the family were thrown once again into panic before it was confirmed it was not Rebecca. *The Big Issue* featured Rebecca as a missing person, the police reacted to sightings and travelled to Scotland and Sheffield, but nothing came of any of it. In 2005, the police informed the family that they were going to say they were looking for a body.

'This was a big shock,' says Lynne. 'We'd always kept on hoping she'd turn up, but they explained that they felt it was very unlikely that she was alive because she would have come back to see Tyler. That was a watershed moment for me to accept and I haven't quite accepted that conclusion yet. But I would like some closure. Sometimes I believe she's alive. Sometimes I have my doubts. But as long as there is no body, no one really knows.'

The police apparently have had phone calls saying Rebecca was shot in someone's garden. But there's been no proof. There have even been rumours that her body is in the woods somewhere. 'I would take the dog for a walk in the woods,' says Lynne, 'and I'd imagine finding her body, or we'd get to the river and I'd think she was in there. It's not right to have to live your life like that.'

While still suffering terribly about Rebecca, Lynne had another shock to contend with. Her father became very ill in 2006. He started to have difficulty breathing because he had problems with his lungs – possibly a condition he'd picked up as a crane driver exposed to the dust from the coal he lifted – and he ended up in hospital, suffering horribly. Suddenly, all Lynne's attention was channelled in her dad's direction. 'I lost my father in 2006, which was a big blow,' she says. 'My dad was always there for me and now he'd gone. He was also very close to Rebecca. That was my one compensation. I thought if Rebecca is no longer with us, at least she is up there now with her granddad and they can look after each other. Strangely enough, that gave me some comfort.'

She found she grew stronger in her attitude towards Rebecca's disappearance. 'Dad was seventy-three and we lost him on 28 April 2006. My mum was so dependent on him. Now I had to take care of her too.' This meant Lynne had to keep herself together for her own mother. So she didn't have so much time to dwell on where Rebecca was and what had happened to her.

Later that year, Lynne and Laura took part in a TV documentary called *Without A Trace*. Lynne went to see a psychic as part of this programme. 'She often helps in police investigations,' says Lynne. 'She got in touch with my dad to see if Rebecca was there, but he reported to her that she wasn't. So that, in a way, brought me no relief. I didn't get any closure but I try to think that no news is good news.'

There is also very welcome news about Tyler: he's had new foster parents and he's getting on really well in his new home. Even better, his foster mother, Anya, used to know Rebecca when she was a little girl. She also lives round the corner from Lynne and she has four other children for Tyler to play with. At last, Tyler is in a good environment and enjoying his childhood.

'Since Christmas 2006, Tyler has been with Anya and her family. He is so settled and it's great,' says Lynne. 'He loves his foster brothers and sisters, plus we get to see him all the time. I take him to school every day and pick him up. Finally, he is somewhere where he can be a little boy again. I'm so relieved. I can also be his nanny again now.'

Also Laura has had some support. 'Laura had some counselling at school,' says Lynne, 'but she's been very pragmatic. I wouldn't have got through this without Laura. She's stronger than me emotionally. Plus she's stricter with Tyler.'

As a family, they devote a lot of time to keeping Rebecca's memory alive. 'My sister-in-law bought me two bright-pink Rebecca roses, which are in the garden, and they are lovely reminders of Rebecca. I take Tyler for walks round the Rebecca bush when he visits,' says Lynne. 'We're doing all sorts of different things. For instance, Anya has made him a collage out of photos of his mum and put it up next to his bed.'

Lynne has also framed lots of different photos of Rebecca and put them around the house. 'I've got several albums of my photos of her. When Tyler comes round, we talk about his mum all the time. There was a phase when one of his social workers disapproved of the family talking about his mum. She thought it was upsetting him. But now we talk to him a lot about his mum. He loves it.'

Soon Tyler will visit the local police station and they'll show him what has been done to find his mum. Lynne is also keeping every newspaper clipping about Rebecca so that, when he's older, Tyler realises how much was done to find her. 'I've got a great picture of me, Rebecca and Laura just before she went,' says Lynne. 'We look so alike. I want Tyler to have all these pictures so he doesn't forget what his mother looks like.'

Lynne has also had a couple of counselling sessions. 'I went to find me again. I sat and cried and told the story of Rebecca going missing and what had happened to me and the family,' she says. 'The therapist did say it might be nice to have a shrine to Rebecca in the house, maybe somewhere with flowers where I could sit and talk to her when I was fed up. He even suggested a memorial service and reminded me that she didn't have to be dead for this to happen, as it would be a celebration of her life. I haven't quite got round to doing those things yet, but it's good to have them there as possibilities.'

Poignantly, when his granddad had been cremated, Tyler wanted to visit him. 'He thought his granddad would have a grave. It was very moving. On the way up there he asked, "I wonder if we'll see Mum's grave up here, Nan,"' says Lynne. 'Tyler had written his granddad a note saying, "I hope you're happy up there in heaven." We went up to the old oak tree where his ashes had been scattered and placed it there. It was very beautiful and very sad at the same time. Tyler was still trying to find some kind of closure around his mum. He wanted to see a grave.'

It's five years since Rebecca disappeared. She is still in all their hearts. The whole family want to make sure that Tyler is content and stable. 'He's had so much to bear,' says Lynne, 'but it's wonderful to see how happy he is running around with his four foster brother and sisters. We'll all keep on being there for him and hoping that still Rebecca might walk in the door one day.'

Tyler has had a terrible time, but at least now he's enjoying his life.

Chapter Five

I Loved My Mum
and Dad but I Missed
My Birth Parents

As a skinny, long-limbed little boy growing up in the suburbs, Peter Rowan developed a strange idea about where babies come from. He thought that in order to have a child, all parents applied to the authorities, that the officials came round and checked out the family, then, if everything was acceptable, they simply received a baby. Forget birth, Peter believed in government-controlled baby shopping.

This belief system was totally understandable because Peter and his younger sister, Wendy, were adopted. And that's the version of their beginnings that they had been told on numerous occasions. John and Mary Rowan, their adoptive parents, were scrupulous about their ethical responsibilities towards their children. They told them the truth about their adoption from the start – they just didn't have a conversation about how other parents came by their children.

In fact, Peter was 11 before he discovered the truth and he

was duly horrified – other parents, it transpired, took their clothes off and had something called sex when they made babies. However, with this realisation a seed was sowed in Peter's mind that was to remain dormant for a few years – somewhere outside his cosy home life were a man and a woman who had created him and these were the people who shared their genes with him.

But at that point, all he knew was that his story began in 1965 when John and Mary were a handsome, 20-something couple – him tall and sporty, her skinny and attractive. They decided to embark on a big adventure far from their home in Surrey. This was the era of £10 tickets to Australia when the land down under needed a workforce. For John and Mary, this was an opportunity to escape, so they grabbed it with both hands and boarded the boat that was to change their lives completely.

They found themselves jobs – in insurance for John and as a secretary for Mary – and a swish new flat overlooking Sydney Harbour. They even got to watch the famous Sydney Opera House being built from their window. Not surprisingly, they fell in love with Australia. The beauty of the harbour, the sunshine, the barbecues and the outdoor existence transformed their lives for the better.

As they became more settled and content, their thoughts turned to having children. But they had to face the fact that Mary wasn't able to conceive naturally and they decided that adoption was the answer. Having passed all the requirements set by social workers, everything was fine, so all they had to do was wait for an available baby.

A year passed before they received that all-important phone

call in 1968. There was apparently a three-week-old baby boy waiting for them at Benalla Hospital, which was 300 miles away. John and Mary were hardly able to believe it was happening as they boarded the train to fetch the child. But it was. There was Peter lying in his cot – a very new baby boy. They were naturally overjoyed. It was a magical time for the Rowans.

As he grew up, Peter was told stories about this first year. One of the main tales was that he was a scrawny baby that his mum fed up and made into a bouncing, healthy boy. It made him feel wanted; it made him feel as though he had a mother who cared for and nurtured him. And it informed his own personal narrative about his life.

Two years later, the Rowan family went through the same adoption rigmarole again. This time, a baby daughter, Wendy, arrived. The manner of her arrival – via the local authorities and hospital – somehow confirmed Peter's version of birth even though he was only two years old. This information was stored in his memory for future reference.

At this point, the family moved from the flat to a much bigger house, ideal for bringing up children, out in the suburb of Narabeen. Although the word 'suburb' gives the wrong impression. This house was built halfway up a cliff and the garden was an acre of bush land. Michael grew up surrounded by wattle trees and multi-coloured parrots. It was an exotic upbringing. And as he got older, his father would take him out bushwalking trips that were to remain with him and inspire him for the rest of his life.

But as the years passed, John and Mary started to miss their close relatives in Hampshire. Now they had children, they realised how wonderful it would be to have grandparents, aunties, uncles and cousins around, because they and the children didn't have that support or that closeness with their friends in Australia. The Rowan family used to visit Hampshire several times a year and, the more they went, the more John and Mary experienced a desire to return home. Mary was also tired of the heat and the sexism. Everything was so divided – they'd go out for dinner and the women would end up in one room and the men in another. She really didn't like this segregation.

However, being the sort of democratic parents that they were, they put this question to 11-year-old Peter and 9-year-old Wendy. Should the family move back to Britain? Peter and Wendy were unanimous in their response. There were no doubts in their minds. Over the years of visiting England, they had built up a romantic image of its possibilities – there were all those old castles, those bluebell woods, those ancient churches. Then there were all those generous relatives there as well. That was the clincher. They wanted to go. So off they all went with all their worldly possessions to Melton in Hampshire. It was to be a huge change for them.

Going to school in Hampshire soon divested Peter of his innocence about sexual matters. He started hearing his classmates use the word 'fuck' rather a lot. So he asked them what it meant. This was 1978 and punk had just happened, so there was that sort of feisty spirit around. 'Oh, it means going to bed with someone,' said one of the boys at his middle school. Peter immediately jumped to the wrong conclusion. He thought it meant literally being in bed or even on the bed with someone. It was a definition that was bound to end in trouble!

The trouble happened when he got home. Some of his parents' friends had visited the day before and he'd seen them sitting on the bed. 'Your friends came round yesterday and fucked,' he said revelling erroneously in his newfound vocabulary. At this point, his parents explained exactly how babies came into being with some useful physiological detail. This was the rude awakening that was ultimately to start him on his journey to find his birth parents. But at this stage, his search was more of a dormant idea that would take another decade to mature.

Surrey did not fulfil Peter's youthful romanticism. Their new house was much smaller than the one they'd had in Australia and the garden was tiny. And school was a nightmare. He was the Aussie newcomer and that meant not fitting in. Academically, he found himself 18 months behind and he got bullied for having an Australian accent. 'Talk Oz,' the kids shouted at him. This affable, big-hearted, tall, skinny kid found himself out of his depth. He also had difficulty with British humour – he just didn't get irony and sarcasm. So the other kids thought he was stupid. Which he wasn't. He was intelligent but unsophisticated. However, he was cast as the outsider and this was a role that was to endure for the next 19 years.

Peter felt different and, frankly, he was different. But neither – and this is a telling trait – did he want to fit in. He had some recognition of his non-conformity even then. He was unhappy with his lot at school, yet fiercely protective of his singularity. The bullying didn't cow him into adapting, it merely shored up his determination to remain different.

Although he did find one genuine friendship during his teenage years and the effect of this friendship was to stay with him. Jim, a tough but also gentle 13-year-old who witnessed the tormentors bullying Peter, decided that he wasn't going to stand there and do nothing. So he took them on. He actually fought the bullies off with his fists. Afterwards, Jim and Peter became firm friends. They went off cycling together, they went fishing together and the quality of Peter's life improved significantly. He had a mate who cared about him and that was all that mattered. The psychological impact of this friendship was profound – Peter learned that he could be different and attract deep friendship too. That was an emboldening lesson for a richer life.

Like many teenagers who are eager to mark their individuality, when he was 15, Peter invented parents that were unlike the ones he had. He imagined that he belonged elsewhere, that he had parents who had vast libraries in a house set on farmland where there were lots of animals. Somewhere along the way, he also started to create a mental picture of the parents who had conceived him. His adoptive parents had dropped into conversation over the years very small pieces of information about his birth parents. These were the bare bones to which he was then mentally adding flesh. His birth father, he learned, was a loner and wanderer, while his mother was very caring. Now he started to merge these fantasies – his birth mother, for instance, would be bookish and his birth father would be an inventor. And there was definitely a farm involved. Peter always dreamed of being a cowboy.

His interior life became vivid, but his exterior one was silent. He didn't share these fantasies. In fact, they fed his solitude. As a 16-year-old, Peter would often sit up old oak trees in the neighbouring hills singing little songs. He'd also actively wonder what it would have been like to spend these years with his original parents in Australia. Would he have felt that he belonged more? Would he have actually lived on that farm?

Gradually, Peter became more and more of a loner. It was as if, by osmosis of the imagination, he had absorbed the idea of his birth dad and he was now becoming him. He would seek solace and freedom in nature. He went for long walks into the hills. Sometimes he even built himself a shelter out of ferns and then slept out. He was actively trying to be embraced by something else bigger than himself, bigger than his present reality at school and home. He passionately wanted to be accepted and enveloped somewhere else, so he looked to nature to provide this comfort. What he was missing in a feeling of roots and real belonging, he was finding in the stones, the trees and the wild animals.

Peter would lie completely still in the bracken with only the stars for company and then be absolutely terrified by the blood-curdling screams of foxes hunting and fornicating. Somehow, this act of being scared transformed him. In the morning, he'd wake up and feel completely in peace and in harmony with his surroundings. By confronting this primal fear, he felt connected to the universe in a way that he secretly longed to be connected to his family and friends. His relationship with nature became his main intimate relationship.

Still unafraid of being considered weird, he took to going off on his own for hours and meditating in nearby fields. John and Mary were getting worried by their son's proclivity for solitude. They even threw a party for him so that he'd find some new friends. But it didn't really work. Peter wasn't really interested in the same things as them. He knew they thought he was strange because they would say things like 'you're deep', but he still didn't feel inclined to change their opinions. Part of him was attracted to the idea of being the outsider.

Peter also started playing the didgeridoo, which only augmented his 'freak' status. He was also developing a growing interest in aboriginal culture and tribes. Much later, on a plane to the US, Peter met an academic who told him that it was common for adopted people to show interest in tribal cultures and their spiritual knowledge. He was told that, instead of being mothered and fathered by their birth parents, they were looking for nurturing from the great mother and father spirits of the earth. This all made complete sense to Peter.

He did start excelling at his schoolwork. And at 18, with good A-levels in maths, physics and English literature, he went off to do a psychology degree at Manchester University. Long-haired, good-looking and possessing an old soul, his life was about to change once again. At university, something novel started to happen. Freed of the shackles of his school reputation, Peter started to attract lots of pretty girl students. He discovered that not only was he considered good-looking, but also charismatic and wise. At last he was sexy.

This was the mid-1980s and there were many poetry gatherings, lots of intense discussions about philosophy, different girlfriends and then there was Sita. Having met her one evening that was full of symbolic messages in precisely the way that satisfied Peter's growing hunger for spiritual serendipity – she was looking for a light for her cigarette and she found him – he fell in love. Sita had big dark eyes, long, long eyelashes and gorgeous hair, and was the daughter of a local Sikh family. They shared the same inventive craziness. Not surprisingly, they were inseparable for the next four years.

Missing

It wasn't a coincidence that Peter fell in love with a British Indian woman. It felt to him as though they both were soul partners in their search for belonging. He felt at home with all her family because they, too, were strangers to England in their hearts. Their outsider status melded with his own. He felt strongly connected to all of them.

And this was to cause some pain at home with his parents, John and Mary. They couldn't help it – they were not keen on Sita. It was a cultural, generational thing. But it meant there were difficulties between Sita and them, and that created a distance between Peter and them. But perhaps he needed this distance to start his real journey to find his birth parents. And it did have a knock-on effect. Sita started encouraging Peter to search for them in Australia.

He also began to fantasise even more about his birth parents and what they might be like. He loved John and Mary deeply but, at a deeper level, he missed his birth parents. He longed to find out where he really came from. But sometimes he felt guilty as well. He knew he was projecting a romantic image onto his birth parents and he was aware that it could all be a total fantasy, and that made him feel uncomfortable.

Occasionally, his mum and dad would ask if he wanted to find out about his birth parents. He'd always go through the same routine. He'd reassure them that he loved them dearly and didn't need to find his birth parents. Underneath, he genuinely wanted to let them know how he really felt, but he also didn't want to hurt them. They'd been supportive parents and he didn't want them to feel unappreciated.

However, there was another growing strand to his fantasy about his origins, and it was that he had aboriginal genes. Student friends at Manchester University had pointed out that he actually had aboriginal features, especially his nose. This idea excited him. A lot. In fact, he even remembered one evening, when he was babysitting as an A-level student, the father of that family had insisted that Peter looked like an aborigine because of his long legs and his broad shoulders as well as his nose. This possibility lay in his mind waiting to be confirmed at a later date.

His eagerness to discover his tribal roots grew. Especially with Sita egging him on. Now living together in London with their degrees finished – Peter got a first in psychology – they went to see a play being produced by an aboriginal cast. They approached the actors at the end and asked if they thought that Peter had aboriginal roots. Afterwards, they all ended up back at the Camden flat where some of the cast were staying. 'What do you think?' said Peter, eager for some sort of acknowledgement. One of the Aboriginal elders must have seen Peter's hunger for his origins and he offered him some healing instead.

This graceful and intriguing old man took out his didgeridoo and started playing it right into Peter's abdomen. The low wailing went right into the seat of his emotions and took him on a sound journey of the soul. These plaintive sounds comforted his feeling of being lost and brought some peace to his increasingly turbulent internal life. A week later, Peter could still feel the sound echoing round his body. It had a deep and long-lasting effect on him. Somehow, it seemed to connect him to himself and confirm who he was. Now from a much more profound and centred place, he decided that he would seek out his birth parents. The healing provided him with the permission to go ahead and try to find them.

It was still to be another few years before Peter went to Australia. By this time, he'd split up with Sita, who'd gone to live in the USA. Peter then started a relationship with a tai-chi teacher called Lisa, whose family came from Malaysia. Now 30, he was himself a tai-chi teacher, and the couple were invited to Australia to do some workshops. Peter made his mind up that he would look for both his parents if the universe gave him the right signs. Always a believer in synchronicity, now he intended to test its powers with regards to his very personal journey.

Amazingly, at the end of their workshop in Melbourne, a participant called Amritsa started talking about her friend who was writing a book about adoption. That was the sign that Peter had been waiting for. It was also a contact who could actually give him the details of what should be done. He filled in the correct forms and settled back to wait. They said it would take up to two months to process. Miraculously – because he only had two weeks left in he country – two days later, he received a letter, which contained the name of his birth mother. He looked at the words – Laura Connolly – again and again. And there was an address. His life was about to change again.

He phoned the adoption helpline and they advised him to write her an ambiguous letter in case she wasn't the only one to read it. He also put in the telephone number of where he would be staying. Over the New Year period of 1997, he and Amritsa travelled to the countryside deep in the bush, where her friend Victoria had a house. A few days later, Victoria answered the phone and whispered to him, 'I think it's your mother.'

He took the phone and found himself having the conversation that he'd dreamed of all these years. 'Is that Peter?' said a shaky voice. He didn't burst into tears. He simply found himself in an almost ethereal state of calm. 'Did you get a letter?' he asked because it seemed the right thing to do. Very quickly, Laura admitted that she had, in fact, started to search for him only a week previously. More serendipity. If he needed any more confirmation that this was the right thing to do, here it was. They arranged to meet up. She also gave him the name of his birth father. It was Joe Wilson. They were both 19 at the time of the pregnancy and had gone their separate ways. She hadn't seen him since.

In the meantime, Amritsa had had a dream saying that she was supposed to drive him up to see his mother. So they set off on the two-day journey and on the way found themselves stopping at an animal orphanage, of all places. Among the orphan wombats and orphan kangaroos, they laughed at the absurdity of the 'orphan' Peter being there, just before he was to meet the mother that gave him up for adoption 30 years earlier.

When they stopped overnight, Peter decided to look up the Wilson families around the area where his birth mother lived, just in case his birth father happened to have stayed in the same area. There were only three in that area phone book so he phoned the first on the list. A woman answered the phone.

She sounds aboriginal, thought Peter to himself, still wondering if that particular fantasy would be true. She told him that Joe was out in the paddock feeding the bullocks and to call back that evening. It looked as though he had succeeded with his first call.

Within hours, he had his potential birth father on the phone. It was all happening at such a giddy pace, he could hardly keep up. 'Do you remember a girl in Moyhu in 1968,' Peter asked, 'when you were an ambulance driver on the Snowy river project?'

Joe did remember. 'Yeah, I do,' he said simply. 'Nice girl, she was.'

'Do you remember that she was pregnant?' asked Peter daringly.

'I do remember something like that,' he answered. Now the momentum was unstoppable.

'Well, that was me and you're my dad,' continued Peter with a dramatic flourish. Joe admitted immediately that he could have been his dad. And Peter was relieved when there were no awkward silences. Afterwards, they just carried on talking as though they'd known each other for years, making a date and time to meet up in the following week.

In fact, as Amritsa and Peter drove up to meet his birth mother, they went along the Snowy River. Historically, it turned out that, around the time of Peter's birth, this river had been changed to flow west rather than east. It was as though it had a symbolic connection with Peter's life, which had also been forced to go west in the direction of Britain, rather than east and Australia.

Peter had entered a profoundly magical state. He was preternaturally calm. Within days, he'd spoken to his birth mother and his birth father. Now he was actually on the way to meet his birth mother. He was incredulous yet had total faith that this was right and happening at the same time. This was his own journey to more of himself and somehow he knew it was going to be a bountiful experience.

The second night's stopover, now near to Moyhu, where Laura lived, presented even more signs. It turned out that Amritsa's friend, Fran, who they were staying with, was, in fact, a good friend of Laura's. She was also very inquisitive about this visit to her friend from this good-looking, long-haired 30-year-old. But Peter was keeping quiet about it because he wanted to protect Laura and also because he didn't want to dilute the experience of this first meeting with his birth mother. He did, however, find out that Laura had two daughters so he knew that he had half-sisters.

Fran was also a healer with a huge country property. So Peter was able to spend the night in a teepee on her land as part of his preparations to meet his birth mother. He wanted to spend some time alone first, bringing himself home before this significant and emotional meeting.

The next morning, Amritsa drove him to the designated meeting place, as she herself had dreamed she would do only the week before. On the way, Peter noticed some highly perfumed white lilies that were growing by the roadside and stopped to pick a bunch of them. As they left, a flock of rainbow-coloured parrots flew overhead. It was as if the landscape itself was acknowledging the importance of this reunion. They found the intersection at Wallan and waited for Laura to arrive. In the past, when he'd imagined this scenario over and over again in his mind, it had been like a scene from a Western and this was pretty close to that picture.

A car pulled up on the other side of the intersection. 'I think it's your mother,' said Amritsa. As if floating in his own dream world, Peter got out at the same time as the woman on the other side of the road. Without words, they found each other and hugged for a very long time, as two people would who had missed each other for their entire lives. Neither of them cried. But Amritsa, who was waiting nearby, burst into unstoppable sobs. She seemed to be doing the crying for both of them.

Unknown to Peter, Laura had plans for another special meeting as well. 'We'll have to drive to Benalla for it,' she said in a voice that conveyed joy and worry simultaneously. 'I don't know how it will go.' Laura was now 46 and she'd lost her son to adoption 30 years earlier.

Peter looked at her as they drove along and he thought she looked beautiful but sad. She had dark hair and hazel eyes and, unlike him at 6 feet, 4inches, she was about 5 feet, 6inches. He couldn't see his own likeness in her, but he could see that their separation had etched itself on her features. This was the deep sadness that he could see in her face.

They drove to Benalla together – together at last. Then she dropped him in the local park, which was right next to the old red-brick hospital where he'd actually been born. He was filled with amazement. He was with the mother who gave birth to him and he was near the hospital where the birth had actually happened.

'I'll go and get your sisters and come back,' she said, allowing herself to cry gently now while he held her. Sisters – he had half-sisters and he wondered what they were like. While she went off into town, he did some tai chi in the park to ground himself and then he decided to take a walk into the hospital. He wandered around the wards and even saw some old incubators out the back and found himself wondering if he'd been in one of them when he was that tiny baby that was just about to be uprooted from his mother.

Eventually, Laura made it back to the park, but was emotional because his sisters had told her they were upset she'd never told them about this brother. And they were shocked. Ever supportive and understanding, Peter calmed her down and they went off to a nearby motel, opened a door and there were two girls staring at him. It didn't take long for them all to dissolve into one big love heap, a hug to end all hugs. Now they were all crying at once. All those powerful feelings of shock, happiness and fear merged together. Half an hour later, they sat down and had a cup of tea together. They couldn't stop looking at one another. They had a hunger to take in any physical resemblance they could find as proof of this fantastic discovery.

Peter's younger sister, Hannah, was 18 and she did look like him. Brown hair and similar facial features. They both held out their hands and the lines were almost identical. After a lifetime of feeling different, Michael was beginning to feel the same. His longing for belonging was finally being fulfilled.

His other sister, Carly, was 21 and usually lived in Melbourne. He didn't look like her but they had other similarities. She'd just written a book about a man who'd swum the river Murray, one of Australia's longest; Michael had just written a book about tai chi with Lisa, his ex-girlfriend. Both Carly and Peter wrote poetry, which turned out to be very similar. Carly has gone on to become a household name in Australia as a TV presenter and comedian.

They had a great time together. It was only slowly, after that initial meeting, that Peter discovered what a huge impact his adoption had on his mother. How he was taken from her as soon as he was born, so she never even saw him or held him. How she had thought about him every day since. And how having a child out of wedlock was such a taboo in Australia during the 1960s that she was treated as a pariah in Moyhu. At 19, she didn't go out for a whole year – she couldn't. She felt too ashamed.

Since that all-important day in February 1968, Laura had said a daily prayer for her missing baby boy. Then, at last, she was reunited with him. Peter stayed for a couple of days with his new family, but was to discover later that Laura was traumatised because he appeared and left again so quickly.

Strangely enough, 30 years on, his birth father, Joe, was actually living an hour away from his birth mother. They hadn't seen each other since they were 19 but they hadn't moved very far away from each other. Peter set off to see him and his family too. He took a train south to Oxley and started looking for someone who could be his father. He saw a short, strong-looking farmer sort marching towards him in a knowing way.

'Hello, are you Peter?' he announced. Peter's brain went into overdrive. Was this that romantic, loner figure he'd always imagined? In fact, his fantasy turned out to be very near the truth.

'Ah, son, it's been a long time,' said Joe as he gave Peter a bear hug. Somehow, these words seemed so right – they provided the homecoming that Peter needed to hear. They were so simple yet so healing. Joe led him to his magnificent 1959 Holden car and Peter was over the moon. But he was to become even more elated. Bernie told him it was this very car where he'd been conceived way back in 1967. He couldn't get much closer to his roots!

Inside the car was a cute little four-year-old boy, Jim, Peter's youngest half-brother. He also had a squashy nose, just like Peter's. His world was becoming rich in similarities now and it was to change his way of thinking. Peter was changing from an outsider into at least a part-time insider. And then Joe dropped a bombshell onto this incipient insider. 'Do you know you're related to Ned Kelly?' he said. 'Ned was your great-uncle – my grandmother was Ned Kelly's sister, Grace.'

This news was incredibly exciting for Peter. His family mythology was even bigger and more outrageous than even he had dared to imagine. He wasn't a fraud after all. Ned Kelly was Australia's most famous outlaw – born in 1855, he was a horse thief who became a bush ranger whose gang carried out daring robberies. His trademark was the home-made armour, which entered Australian iconography. He was hanged in 1880 and has been thoroughly romanticised as a rebel who thought he could live beyond the law. That Peter was related to him fed into his own personal mythology.

What was more, 56-year-old Joe turned out to be an irrepressible character too. He was not just a farmer but a genuine eccentric as well. He was the birth father that Peter had imagined. In the flesh. And he lived in the same ramshackle farmhouse that his grandmother – yes, Ned Kelly's sister – had lived. Ned had sat on the very bed that they still had in the bedroom. Peter was totally thrilled that his background was so fascinating and layered with rebel history.

The farm itself was littered with ancient vehicles and farm machinery – Joe was always planning to fix them. There were big iron locomotives, cars and ploughs. It was a museum of rapidly deteriorating vehicles and machines from the past.

At this point, Peter was in awe of the eccentricity but also a little worried that he wouldn't be able to communicate with Joe. He may be my dad, he wondered to himself, but will I really be able to talk to this hillbilly in blue overalls with a big smile and only two teeth? He needn't have worried. Joe didn't just have sparkling blue eyes in his weathered face, but an easy warmth and great sense of humour too.

He didn't mince his words either. Amid the 1930s kitchen furniture, the old, old wooden floor and the picture of the Last Supper hanging above the table, sun streamed in the kitchen window onto Joe's face. 'Son, I've had a hard life,' he said and Peter knew how real his words were.

At the same time, this was the most real that Peter had ever felt. He'd never felt so comfortable in his body and who he was. He thought to himself, this is a time that I'm going to remember for the rest of my life.

Joe's wife, Mel, was wonderful to Michael as well. She had three children with Joe: Jim, Michael and Kate. In fact, she was from the Philippines rather than being aboriginal as Michael had initially thought when he'd heard her on the phone. Not all his heritage fantasies had been true – not that one. Not that it mattered now.

During his two-day stay at the farm, Peter did find out some other bits of information about his birth parents' relationship. Joe had been in love with Laura and, when she got pregnant, he had wanted to marry her. Gradually, it emerged that he was still angry and bitter about her rejection of him.

Peter also discovered that Laura had been in a near-fatal car crash when she had been six months pregnant with him. 'You were definitely meant to be,' she would say to him much later. Joe had even joined the priesthood at one point because he'd felt there was a curse on him. Laura rejected him, then three girlfriends died one after the other. The priesthood didn't last long though. 'It was full of "yes" men,' he told Peter contemptuously.

Not long after Peter arrived at the farm, Joe took him out into the paddock and announced, 'Let's see if you can crack a whip.' Hampshire-bred and Manchester University-educated Peter found himself with a manly challenge on his hands. But he managed to convince Joe that he could do it. Joe then took him off on his motorbike around his land. At that moment, Joe recalled a childhood memory that he used to have – which was of an old man taking him on a motorbike around a farm. He wondered whether it had been an example of a future memory?

Joe made things too. Like hovercrafts. Apparently, he'd got hold of the plans from the inventor in the US and then spent time carving the propellers out of wood and sewing the skirts for them. Joe was not your run-of-the-mill dad, that's for sure. And Peter loved that.

When Peter met Pat, Joe's brother, his DNA puzzle fell into place. 'He was the same build as me,' says Peter, 'and the same height at 6 feet, 4 inchs and had the same Cheshire-cat smile. That felt really good, finding a man who really looked like me.'

A week later, Peter managed to get Laura and Joe together and take photographs of all three of them. Peter finally felt whole. 'It was incredibly validating,' he says, 'to know that I had a mother and father in Australia and that I wasn't just making up ideas about them. They were real and they made me feel so much more real. I felt, and continue to feel, a sense of contentment and peace that I'd never felt before. Before I found Joe and Laura, I always felt as though I was floating just above the ground. Now I feel as though my feet are firmly planted on the earth. There's nothing missing any more.'

Ten years on, Peter has returned to Australia. He lives with his wife, Shelley, and his two children, Lilly, six, and Ned, four, in Miami, Queensland. His children have four sets of grandparents and all those cousins too. They have an incredible extended family, thanks to Peter's successful search for his birth parents.

(All names in this story have been changed)

Chapter Six

My Son Did Not Run Away From Home

Nicki Durbin is adamant. Her cheeky-faced, kind, 19-year-old, son, Luke, did not run away from home. One of the last CCTV images of Luke shows him in Ipswich, Suffolk, in the early hours of 11 May 2006. He's trying to sweet-talk one of the local cab drivers into giving him a free lift to the village of Hollesley, where he lives with his mother and 18-year-old sister, Alicia.

The cab driver refused. After all, he was trying to make a living. Nicki is eager to point out that she doesn't blame him for not taking her son. She wouldn't have given him a lift if she had been that cab driver. However, in retrospect, she feels his decision is laced with the terrible sadness of knowing that Luke never made it home. In fact, there is another CCTV image showing Luke walking to the bus station. And then... nothing else. Luke has never been seen again. It's as if a giant hand came down and removed him from this earth. There have been no confirmed sightings of him since.

Rumours, of course, abound. Nicki, 38, who has been through such awful grief in the last year not knowing where her much-cherished son is, hears them last of all. But she does hear them. There have been stories about a body being found in a freezer and a headless corpse being discovered in a field nearby, but the most persistent rumour is that Luke has run away.

The reason Nicki feels so strongly about this particular theory is that Luke had already left home once before. However, he was in contact every day and it was only three days before he was on the phone asking if it was OK to come home. He did not disappear. He did not go missing without telling anyone. 'We weren't getting on well at that time. There were disagreements about him not being responsible about work and being lazy. He was 18, it was February 2005 and he left a letter and a rose,' says dark-haired, slim Nicki with a smile. 'The letter said he'd got to go away and find himself but that he'd stay in touch and that no one could be a better mum than me.'

Luke, who had dropped out of his Colchester college because it was too far away to commute, went off to France that time. 'He was in Calais and he phoned to let us know,' she says. 'He arrived home looking really sheepish and it was lovely to have him back. We laughed at all his stories. Mind you, he did come home looking like Dick Whittington. He had his skateboard in a black bin liner, he looked in a sad state but it was comical at the same time. He'd even swapped cuddly toys with Alicia, so he had her sheep tied on his backpack too. That shows how close they are as brother and sister.'

-'s argument is that Luke is the sort of son who wouldn't

leave home without letting the family know. Even when there were tensions in the household, he kept in touch and let her know how much he loved her. Nicki Durbin is a single mother who is extremely close to both her children, not least because they've had to fight so hard to survive financially. It hasn't been easy, she explains, but their life together has been rich in terms of affection and simplicity. Now he's missing and he hasn't let them know where he is, so Nicki is certain that he hasn't run away.

Luke was not a planned baby. Nicki Durbin's father was in the RAF, which meant the family moved around a lot as children. Nicki changed schools a lot over the years and it wasn't easy for her. 'I didn't cope well with changing schools and friends,' she says. 'I found it difficult to fit in, so I became rebellious. I turned myself into a teenage punk. I had spiky black hair and wore far too much black make-up. I'd found a crazy way of fitting in. My parents handled it very well – they didn't freak out. One evening, I remember we had to go for dinner at the officer's mess. I turned up in my punk outfit and they coolly took me with them, without saying a word. They had a good handle on my rebellion psychologically. They knew if they became stricter, I'd rebel more. They were right.'

However, Nicki had already met Carl, a fellow rebel and punk. 'I was fifteen when I started going out with him,' she says. 'I'd already given up with school really. I couldn't do the options that I wanted, so I lost faith in it. I was seventeen when I found out that I was pregnant. I didn't realise I was pregnant for months. I'd taken the pregnancy test and it had come back negative. I was shocked when I discovered I was four months. I told my mother first and she wasn't at all impressed at first but, after the initial shock, both my parents were surprisingly good about it. I already knew that I didn't want to have an abortion and Carl was keen to be a father, so I went ahead and had Luke despite our youth.'

Giving birth at 17, on 4 December 1986, caused a transformation in Nicki's personality. 'I literally changed overnight,' she says. 'My reality had shifted and I became responsible for another life. Luke was a perfect baby, he didn't have any shrivelled skin. The only trouble was that he had very bad colic, which was hard.' Nicki, Carl and baby Luke moved into a basic bedsit not far from her parents' house in Hollesley. Unfortunately, it was in an attic with no insulation and 1986 was a very cold winter. 'It snowed, we didn't have a bath or a shower and Luke was suffering with colic,' she says. 'It was a nightmare and, in the end, we moved into my parents' bungalow for a month so at least we were warm.'

Eventually, they managed to get a little house in nearby Felixstowe through the council. 'We were very lucky,' she says. 'I was only eighteen and it was a lovely little house. Carl was working as a labourer and he sorted out the garden for Luke to play in.' Within a year, Nicki was pregnant with daughter Alicia. 'Carl was a very good dad. He made time for them,' she says. 'But we grew apart over time because we'd met when we were so young. But it was a very happy time with the children. I felt as though I learned so much from them. Luke was amazingly agile. He was already riding a bike without stabilisers when he was only three, although he also had a lot of accidents. One of the worst days of my life was when Luke broke his leg skidding across the floor. He had to spend Christmas in traction in hospital and I was trying to look after Alicia as well, who was only six months old. That was terrible for all of us.'

By the time Luke was six, his parents had split up and Nicki had moved near to Woodbridge in order to be closer to her parents and sister. 'I felt free and I loved it,' says Nicki. 'But I had two small children and no money. I managed our finances in a very frugal way. For instance, I'd freeze a loaf into three sections. I was very careful. It was a simple but lovely life. Best of all, I had my friends and family living nearby, which meant a lot to me and the kids.'

Nicki was cleaning houses and working in a bar to make ends meet. 'I didn't want to give my children the message that it was all right not to work,' she says, 'so I found little jobs that I could fit in around their school time.' Luke did well at his tiny village primary school in nearby Bawdsey. He was in the football team and was competitive academically. 'There was a great headmistress and Luke excelled there because it was so small,' says Nicki. 'When he went, he didn't have very much self-confidence, but it grew while he was there. It was like a big family for him. There was also a brilliant teacher there called Mr Duncan, who was passionate about bird-watching, and he would take his pupils out at 4am to go on bird trips. Luke loved spotting different birds and, when he got older, he would get me to take him to locations where rare birds had been seen. This teacher inspired him. Luke was tuned into nature. He was always rescuing pigeons and helping cats out. He was always very kind. Even then, Luke had many facets and I really think it was privilege to know him, even though he's my son.'

High School in Woodbridge was a shock. It was enormous in comparison with Luke's little primary school, with over a thousand students. 'He was lost at first but he adapted. He's always been quick witted,' says Nicki. 'And then he became the class joker. He was also developing his charm. Luke is a really sociable person and he is like a magnet for other people. Everyone wants to know him, so he made a lot of new friends quickly.' Luke also started to play the guitar and committed himself to playing well. 'He and a couple of friends played in a rock evening at the school,' she says, 'and he got up and played. He was only in year seven. It takes guts to perform at that kind of young age. He was only twelve and all the sixth formers went. He was great – he wrote his own lyrics and songs. Luke was really into music and after that event, lots of people were coming up to him and congratulating him.'

Academically, Luke, like many teenage boys, thought he could get away with doing very little. 'He was very charming and cheeky,' says Nicki. 'When it came to his GCSEs, he wasn't doing much studying and I thought he was going to do very badly. But four months before the exams, he started revising. He also had a teacher who became his mentor for the GCSEs and she helped a lot. He actually pulled it off and did well. Luke's always been good at retaining information.'

Luke left school and went to college in Colchester in order to study music technology. 'He wanted to study music but he was only sixteen and it took an hour and a half to get there,' says Nicki. 'It just didn't work. It was too tiring for him and he gave that course up after a year. He wanted to play music but he didn't really want to do the theory. He had been working in local restaurant kitchens at weekends. Now he continued to earn some money like that. He didn't really know what he wanted to do.'

At first, Luke was reliable at work, but then he started to be lazy and it caused huge arguments at home. 'I've always been the sort of person who doesn't expect something for nothing,' says Nicki. 'I expect to work and I thought I'd instilled this idea into my children. I'd been working for years at the local library during this period. So I didn't understand what was happening to Luke. He'd always been so respectful and now he was rude and surly. We'd always been such a close threesome. Now there was a lot of tension in the house.'

He wanted a motorbike to get to and fro between shifts in Woodbridge, but Nicki couldn't afford to buy him one. Luke was exhausted and then he seemed to stop working. He was 17 and smoking too much cannabis. It was affecting his motivation, his moods and his relationships with his sister and mother. 'It felt as if he thought he had the right to do nothing,' says Nicki, 'and that was just not acceptable in my eyes. We had a lot of arguments over his attitude. I felt resentful that I'd been struggling for so long to bring my kids up and now Luke wasn't willing to contribute anything. That made me angry.'

It was in February 2005 that 18-year-old Luke decided to go to France and sort his head out. He knew he was messing up his relationship with the mother he loved very much, so off he went to find himself. He didn't go missing. He didn't disappear. Luke just took off for a couple of days to Calais, then thought better of it. Of course, Nicki and Alicia were both overjoyed to have Luke back at home. He may have been acting like a difficult adolescent then but they loved him and wanted their 'old' Luke back.

And their 'old' Luke did come back. He appreciated home again and everything was wonderful until a couple of weeks later when one of their close friends and neighbours died suddenly. 'It was very unusual. I was out and Luke was at home,' says Nicki. 'He was actually making me a Mother's Day card when there was a phone call from an ex-partner of Bob's, saying he couldn't get hold of him. Luke went round to the house and found Bob dead. It was awful. I really regret not being there instead of him. I hate the idea of Luke having to deal with a dead body at his age.'

The situation at home deteriorated. 'He was being disrespectful again,' she says. 'Sometimes I'd look at him and wonder who was occupying my son's body. He had no focus. We'd have huge bust-ups and I would try to calmly "start afresh" and be nice to him. But it would only last ten minutes before he'd drive me mad again. Then he'd tell me that I was over-reacting, which would make me even more cross. He'd talk about moving out and I'd think that was really the only option. I couldn't stand him doing nothing. He was always around the house but he wasn't helping me. I couldn't help feeling as though he was freeloading.'

Just before Christmas 2005, Luke packed his bags and went to stay with friends for a couple of days. He didn't run away, but he did go away, wanting to think about his life and where it was going. 'But he was back after three days and, in the New Year, he really did change,' says Nicki. 'Suddenly, he started helping around the house and looking for work. It was as if he'd decided to get himself together. In the past, he'd always had goals like saving up for a guitar, then achieved them. Luke was back in that frame of mind again. He was talking about going off travelling and recording his songs in a studio and then a job came up in Aldeburgh, which was working in the restaurant that was next to a deli. That was just great for him. He was very happy about it.'

Transport was an issue because it was taking him too long to travel by bus. Nicki's parents helped out by giving Luke a loan to buy a motorbike. 'All the shouting and disagreements stopped,' she says. 'Luke would work, then cook us supper. It was delightful. He was such an interesting person; I'd love having him around. Alicia and he were always very close; now they were even closer. I was working for a company who did cottage lettings in Suffolk and that was going well too. The household was harmonious again at last.'

Despite their difficult times, Nicki had always kept faith that her son would pull through and he did. 'Luke and I had a rough ride,' she says, 'but I always knew he was a good lad underneath. Above all, he was kind. I'll never forget when he was eighteen, one of Alicia's friends died of a brain tumour and there was a memorial event to celebrate this boy's life. Some of the kids were in a band and were about to start playing, when one of the boys couldn't get his guitar tuned. Luke simply walked on stage and tuned it for him. He didn't make a big deal about it. He just did it. That was Luke. He could have put his hands in the air and got a big cheer, but he didn't. I was so proud of him.'

At home, Luke was back to being his old considerate self. 'It felt like we'd entered a new chapter,' says Nicki. 'He had a motorbike accident but wasn't hurt. I came back from seeing a friend in Spain and I knew something with him was wrong over the phone. But he'd been lucky – he only had minor injuries. When I walked in, he gave me a huge hug. He was so glad to see me, it was so lovely.'

Two weeks later, on 11 May 2006, in the afternoon, the three of them were in the kitchen together. Luke was planning his night out with friends on his mobile, while Nicki and Alicia were chatting. 'I remember he was laughing so much as he talked. He looked so happy,' she says. 'But little did I realise that was to be the last time I'd see him. That night in the early hours, Luke disappeared.'

Nicki knew Luke was going to stay with a friend that Thursday night so she didn't worry. On the Friday, she phoned his mobile but it was turned off and she assumed that he was at work. 'Even on Friday evening, I went out in Woodbridge, completely unaware that there was a problem,' she says. 'I saw Alex, who was one of the friends he was with, but I didn't realise he hadn't stayed with him or that his motorbike was still parked round at Alex's place. That night I wasn't concerned at all. I'd always thought if anything happened to one of my children, I would know. Well, I didn't.'

On the Saturday, Nicki thought Luke was at work. It was Alicia who had an idea that something wasn't right. She'd talked to Luke's friend Alex the night before and realised that her brother hadn't stayed with him. 'I phoned his workplace and his boss was a little frosty because she thought Luke had let her down,' says Nicki. 'He hadn't gone into work and that's when I started to panic. Luke loved working for her. I think he felt as though she saw his potential because she had trusted him with the keys to the place. But there she was on the other side of the phone saying, "I've got a business to run and Saturday is our busiest day," and I was mortified. I knew that something was seriously wrong.'

Nicki phoned all Luke's friends. Everyone said they hadn't seen Luke since Thursday night. 'I was hit by complete terror,' she says. 'I phoned round the hospitals but he wasn't there. I phoned his friend Alex, who said Luke's motorbike was still parked outside his house. I found out what had happened that night earlier on. Three of them had gone to Zest, a nightclub in Ipswich, together, but Alex had gone home early and Zak, the other boy, lost Luke in the club later on. He went to buy them some drinks and Luke wasn't there when he got back. So they left separately. I phoned the police and they immediately took me very seriously, because it had been over 48 hours since he'd gone missing. They sent someone over within an hour and my nightmare began.'

Of course, half of Nicki was thinking that her Luke would turn up at any time and that she would just give him the biggest telling off that he'd ever had in his life. 'But I knew every time that he'd gone off before, he had let me know what he was doing,' she says. 'It wasn't like him to just disappear. That Saturday is a blur. On the Sunday, the police phoned me to warn me in case the press got wind of it that they were sweeping the river in Ipswich because the nightclub, Zest, where Luke and his friends spent the evening, was next to the river.'

It meant one thing – the police were checking to see if Luke's body was in the water. Nicki hadn't even got used to the idea that her son was really missing yet and then she had to take on board the idea that he might be dead. 'I've never been in that kind of state in my life before,' she recalls. 'I remember just screaming and screaming in the back garden. I was like a banshee. I completely lost it. I couldn't stop because I was in such emotional turmoil.'

Luke's body wasn't found in the river. That news, at least, was a temporary relief. But Nicki was going through lots of different emotions about her missing son. 'I had huge outbursts of anger with Luke,' she says honestly. 'I was angry with him for doing this to his family. One minute, I was ninety per cent sure that he would not just go off and leave us and then I'd get so angry with him for doing just that. I'd be thinking, How could you do this to us? I was hysterical. My emotions from grief to anger were uncontrollable. I had to go along with whatever was going on for me – I had no choice. One minute I was angry, the next sad, the next hopeful.'

Within a few days, life as she had known it was utterly transformed. Peace disappeared. Hell appeared. 'My parents came over,' she says, 'and I ended up telling them I needed to go to bed. It was a comfort just to have them there, but I needed to be in my own space and just go through what I was going through. They would also phone me and check to see if I was OK all the time. It helped knowing they were in the background. I have a handful of close friends and there was Pat who I could really be me with during this period. It was a crazy situation and I was crazy. I didn't mind Pat seeing me like that. Also, one of my oldest friends, Cathy, lives in Australia so it was comforting to be able to ring her at 2am our time, when I was awake with lots of horrible thoughts going around my head.'

For the first month, Nicki was in shock. She took a week off work sick. 'At first, my employers were sympathetic,' she says. 'I wasn't in a state to work. I tried but I couldn't. I spent a lot of time in my bedroom alone. My parents might be downstairs and I'd derive a little bit of comfort from even hearing the television on. It would remind me that normality was still there somewhere. I remember it raining endlessly and all I could think is that it might be raining on Luke's body – that was just so unbearable. It was a very tough time.'

Pat and Nicki put posters up in Woodbridge and they sent out a chain email. Then the CCTV footage arrived at the police station. 'I had to go in and look at it,' says Nicki. 'I was looking at lots and lots of images of young people going into the nightclub, Zest. It was exhausting. You only have to blink and you've missed something. I was looking at people being searched and I saw an arm. It was the way it was held up. Luke was so graceful. You just know your children's mannerisms so well, I was sure it was his arm. That was it, I just saw my son's arm.'

Alex, Zak and Luke had been drinking at a bar in Woodbridge before going to the club. After just half an hour, Alex had already had enough. He went home. Later on, Zak went to the bar to get some drinks and he couldn't find Luke when he came back. They left separately. The CCTV footage showed Luke trying to persuade a taxi driver near the club to take him home without paying. He didn't succeed but he's seen laughing afterwards and shaking his hand. 'I don't blame him for not giving Luke a lift,' says Nicki. 'He shouldn't have done. Luke is looking very relaxed and enjoying himself. He has had a few drinks but he's not drunk. The last image of Luke is at 4am and he's walking towards the bus station. He was obviously trying to get home. That's the last confirmed sighting of him.'

Luke loved a band called the Foo Fighters and they happened to be playing in Ipswich a few weeks after Luke went missing. Nicki and a group of friends handed out posters about Luke at the gig. Flyers were given out and posters put up all over the centre of town but nothing was reported back. It was soul destroying.

Nicki couldn't bear not doing something proactive to find

her son. So she went to the doctor and took a week's sick leave. When she asked for an extension on this, her doctor very willingly gave her one and she took off three weeks in total. But work became very difficult. In October, five months after Luke went missing, she was made redundant.

Once extremely close, Alicia and Nicki started to shut each other out of the anguish they were both feeling about Luke's disappearance. 'We were both trying to protect each other from what we were really thinking,' she says. 'We were practical with one another but we didn't mention what we thought might have happened to him. We weren't dealing with the nitty-gritty, so it was getting very tense in the house. Also, I was aware that I was spending so much time focusing on Luke and that Alicia might feel totally excluded. Her school was really good; she had her AS levels looming and they said it was fine if she couldn't do them this year. I felt so guilty that she was worrying about her brother being dead or alive when she should have been concentrating on her exams. It was horrible but, in the end, we had a real heart-to-heart and cleared the air.'

There are always new stories going around locally about what has happened to Luke. Which is horrendous for Nicki. 'It gets back to me two or three months afterwards,' she says. 'There was the rumour going round that the police had found a headless body in a field and that it was Luke. It wasn't. There was the rumour that he'd joined the Foreign Legion. He hadn't. There is always a new one going round, but they are all complete rubbish. Oh yes, there was another one about his dad holding him hostage. All completely ridiculous.' There was even one about his dad harbouring him.

There was one sighting that got a lot of coverage and it made

Nicki very annoyed. Luke was supposed to have been seen in a blue car with a man who was black. 'There were serious flaws in this story,' says Nicki. 'For a start, Luke didn't have many black friends, purely because Woodbridge is a predominantly white area. The press were issued with a press release from the police, so it became as if he wasn't really missing. This information gave the impression that Luke had just gone off with a bunch of friends. I was furious because it was misleading and it meant attention went away from the fact that my son was missing. It should have been ruled out immediately. The police lost valuable time at this juncture.'

Over the past year, Nicki has been through every emotion. She has experienced little highs when something hopeful happens and hundreds of lows. However, she has been consistent in aiming to keep Luke's name high on the police's list and also in the media. If anyone anywhere knows anything, she will find out. As a mother, it has been unbearable. She doesn't know how she's survived. Sometimes, it's only knowing that she must keep looking for her son which keeps her alive.

The murder of the young sex workers on the streets of Ipswich just before Christmas 2006 also sent terror into Nicki's heart. 'Those girls went missing within a two-mile radius of where Luke disappeared and they were subsequently found murdered,' she says. 'They had something in common with him. They were all willing to get into a car late at night with someone that they didn't know. I was petrified that they would find Luke's body then, but they didn't. When it was going on, all the police attention was focused on finding this murderer. Understandable, but I couldn't stand it. My missing son wasn't getting their time – that made me anxious and frustrated.'

At the end of March 2007, an old school friend of Luke's said she'd seen him in London. 'She'd been to see a show in the West End and, afterwards, she said she saw Luke walk by,' says Nicki. 'She said she was eighty per cent sure it was him and, of course, I want to believe her. I just am not sure whether it was Luke. We went up to London and put up posters, but there is a part of me that accepts it might not have been him. She didn't actually speak to him. In fact, I went on the Jeremy Vine show on Radio 2 around this time, which was really good, but no sightings came out of it and that was utterly devastating for me. The police didn't get one call.'

Nicki put all her energy into the anniversary of Luke's disappearance. It took place on 13 May 2007, in a cinema in Woodbridge, and went very well. It was hosted by John McCarthy, the journalist who was held hostage for five years. 'Local bands played and we had a silent auction,' says Nicki. 'The proceeds went to the charity Missing People.'

A year of missing Luke has taken Nicki on a bumpy ride. 'I'm totally up and down,' she says. 'I don't know if I believe he's alive. Sometimes I do and sometimes, I don't. One day I can keep it together, other days I can't. Yesterday, I went to get some oil and someone asked me if there was any news about Luke. I crumbled and cried. Alicia is different. She's decided to believe that he is still alive.'

One small comfort is that Nicki is in contact with other parents of missing sons and daughters. 'We talk over the phone sometimes,' she says, 'and we can say all the terrible things we can't say to anyone else. We can talk to each other about the darker side of dealing with a missing child. We also write each other emails and the joy of having the internet means you can write really bleak emails to each other. I couldn't write that sort of thing to anyone else. Only someone who is going through it would understand.' Nicki thinks about wanting to possess a part of Luke's body if he is found dead. It sounds crazy but what she means is that she just wants a piece of Luke to be with her for the rest of her life.

Nicki Durbin is a brave, strong mother and she refuses to be a victim. At the moment, she's working as a gardener, but she sees herself getting back into other work soon. She knows she will go on fighting for herself and her daughter. She doesn't know what has happened to her darling son, Luke, but she is convinced of one thing. 'Luke did not run away,' she says again and again. She clings onto to this perspective with the vice-like grip of a mother who will never stop loving her beautiful son.

www.findluke.com

Chapter Seven

I Didn't Know if My Little Girl Was Dead or Alive

Meta Belhaj was recently taken out for lunch at Claridges to celebrate her 57th birthday. It was a very special treat and she relished the luxury of it. She is the first to admit that her life has been tough, and that is an understatement – although she would never focus on that hard aspect.

Another wonderful surprise arrived on Mother's Day. It was a card from her 20-year-old daughter, Nadia. In it, Nadia had written a poem, which caused soft tears of pain and joy to well up in Meta's eyes. 'On the front of the card, there was a picture of a little girl with her foot on her mother's foot and that's what she used to do with me,' says Meta. 'Inside, she'd written that she wanted me to know how much she loves me and that she is grateful for having me in her life. She also put a line about thanking me for raising her alone.' It was a poignant acknowledgement of a daughter's love for her mother. Six years ago, Nadia wouldn't have written that card because their relationship was very different.

Nadia was brought up in Leigh-on-Sea, Essex. It's an old-fashioned town with cockle sheds and cobbled lanes. There are lots of little art galleries, junk shops and quaint bars. It's like going back to the 1950s. The family lived in a three-bedroomed house some ten minutes from the sea. Meta retains the surname Belhaj but her partner, Osama Belhaj, left a long time ago. Meta has brought her children up on her own and all four of them are now grown up: Niki is 36, Samantha 34, Tarik 25 and Nadia 20. Fortunately, dark-haired and handsome Meta Belhaj is a strong woman, because she's had to be. Her husband, Dave, who she met when she was 18, died when Niki and Samantha were little.

She met Osama Belhaj, a Libyan gentleman with whom she had her son, Tarik. He went back to Libya when Tarik was two. Finally, she met Nadia's father, Kevan, who went off to be a waiter on the *Queen Elizabeth 2* when Nadia was three. He never came back to live with them. Meta didn't know how to choose men that would take good care of her; that wasn't part of her education.

Meta herself was one of nine children and she was born in Luton, Bedfordshire. 'When I was two, my mother left our father with four of us. She couldn't cope. Now when I think about it, I wonder now how she could have done that. We went into care,' she says. 'I ended up with a brother in a children's home in Gerrard's Cross. I stayed there until I was four, then I was fostered by a family, where I was told to call the couple mummy and daddy. I thought they were my new parents. But when I was six, they took me back to the children's home. Of course, I thought they didn't want me, which was not a good feeling for a six-year-old to have.

'I stayed at the home until I was fifteen. It was harsh regime with a matron; we didn't get cuddles. We were on our own if we fell over. This matron was very strict if we misbehaved. But there was one lady on the staff that I remember being kind to me. She taught me to knit. And we'd all go on holiday together once a year to places like Cromer in Norfolk. We had fun then and looked forward to that all year.'

Meta explains that she was always fishing for information about her mother at the children's home and, when she was 15, the matron asked if she would like to meet her. 'There was this ritual every Saturday where people would come to the home to take children out to tea. The matron gave me the choice of going out to tea or going to Canvey Island to see my mother. Of course, I chose the latter. Off I went to Canvey Island with a welfare officer but it was horrendous. My mother was so cold. I was so excited about meeting her. She said "Hello" and that was about it. It was very uncomfortable.'

Yet Meta still found herself going to live with her mother when she was 15. Somehow she thought it might work out. It didn't. Meta wanted to be a telephonist but her mother insisted that she take on work binding books in a factory. 'I hated it,' says Meta. 'Everyone seemed so common to me. They all swore a lot. I'd been protected from this kind of life in the children's home. I felt very isolated. I also tried to find out about my father but she wouldn't tell me anything about him. At one point, I found a photo album and there was a picture in there of a man I thought had the same eyes as me. I asked her and she smiled. For a short time, I thought it was my father, then I discovered it was a photo of King George V. I was devastated. My mother died fifteen years ago and she still refused to give me any information about him, like his date of birth or his birthday. I still really want to find him.'

Meta didn't have anything in common with her mother so it was hard work living with her. She dreamt about escaping to Spain and working as an *au pair* but that was not to be. Events took over. One night, she went out to a dance in Southend and met a young man called Dave. He came from South Wales. Innocent and 19, Meta got pregnant soon after they met.

'He was a nice bloke but he had a drink problem,' she says. 'But I didn't know any better and I wanted to get away from my mother. I had my first daughter, Niki, with him and the second one, Samantha.' Then he started getting violent and Meta was beaten so badly on one occasion, he ended up in a police cell. Finally, she left him. Meta didn't get much education in the children's home about men, sex, or love, so she had to find out for herself the hard way.

After Dave was killed in a car accident, things didn't work out with Tarik's father. Then Kevan disappeared to work on the *QE2* when Nadia was three. Meta told Nadia that her dad was working, rather than that he wasn't ever coming back. She was trying to be kind. It just didn't turn out that way.

Recently, Meta has realised what a profound affect unwittingly not telling the truth to the three-year-old Nadia actually had. 'Her father went off to work on a cruise ship and he also left us at that point,' says Meta, 'but I told her that her daddy had gone off to work, which gave her the wrong impression. He then went to live in Japan. For a long time, little Nadia had the idea that her dad was away working, but that he was going to return at some time in the future. She didn't realise he and I had separated. It wasn't until she was about ten that she finally worked it all out. At the time, I didn't think about it. Now I've reflected on what happened and can see it affected her emotionally as a daughter. She didn't know why he wasn't home with us after he'd finished working, so she was missing him as the same time as being confused by his disappearance.'

Nadia was a beautiful little girl with corkscrew hair and big blue eyes. 'She always went to bed early,' says Meta, 'and her primary school teachers said she was a pleasure to teach. She loved going to school. Her bedroom was always neat and tidy. As she got older, she'd come along and help me work as a waitress. She'd fold the serviettes and smile a lot. She was no trouble.'

Meta provided entertainment at the restaurant – at 38, when she'd given up on finding a decent, long-term partner, she took up bellydancing as it gave her a lot of pleasure. Nadia would come along to the Sunday shows. 'There were four women in our troupe. We did shows in restaurants all over Essex,' she said. 'Nadia loved to come along when she could. It was exciting for her. I think she liked seeing her mother performing.'

But inside her lovely little head, Nadia had the words 'Daddy is coming back to live with us' going round and round. She carried the disappointment of realising the truth with her for a long time afterwards. She was haunted by the idea of her missing dad.

At first, when Nadia got to secondary school, everything went well. 'I used to go to their open evenings,' says Meta, 'and they used to say, "She's such a good girl, she's lovely." She liked doing everything.' But Nadia's school life changed when she was 11. 'There were a lot of changes going on in her home life,' says Meta. 'Tarik was leaving home to join the RAF, plus Niki was moving to Cyprus because her husband was also in the RAF and they were going to be stationed there. Then on top of all this, her best friend at school got a boyfriend and Nadia felt rejected.'

By the time she was 12, Nadia was drifting at school and feeling left out. 'All of a sudden, no one at school seemed to like her,' says Meta. 'There were arguments. One particular girl was giving Nadia a hard time. She was being bullied. It was lonely for her. This one girl would wait outside the school gates for her and threaten her. We told the school about it and they said they were dealing with it. But they weren't.'

As a defensive measure, Nadia started hanging out with a new group of friends. 'Nadia's behaviour transformed in a bad way,' says Meta. 'She wouldn't come straight home from school any more; she'd be home by 6pm. I'd ask her where she'd been but she wouldn't tell me. It wasn't like her. She always came home for tea. Now she wasn't doing that. I started to worry about her.'

And the situation with Nadia got worse. She was hanging out with boys. She was going out to clubs and she was coming home late at night. Her mother couldn't control her. 'I told her she couldn't go to the disco unless I came and met her, but she went anyway,' says Meta. 'Her life was now going seriously wrong. She was in with a crowd that I didn't like, but I knew I couldn't choose her friends for her. She'd be coming home at midnight and I'd be frantic. But she still did really sweet things like send me notes telling me that she was really sorry afterwards and that she wouldn't do it again.'

The only trouble was, she did. It was as if Nadia was being torn in half. One part of her – the part that loved her mother

– wanted to be good and she knew what that meant, and the other part – the part that feared being bullied and left out – wanted to be in a gang where she felt safe, even if the gang included teenagers she wouldn't have hung around with before. Nadia started staying out the whole night.

That's when her poor mother, fraught with anxiety about her 13-year-old daughter and what she was doing, used to called the police. 'I couldn't stand it,' says Meta. 'It was making me ill. The police would turn up and take the details about her behaviour. When she got home, they spoke to her and told her to tow the line. This happened a couple of times.' Sadly, it didn't make any difference to her behaviour. Nadia was stuck in a groove. 'The police had her down as a regular,' she says, 'so when Nadia did eventually turn up, they said something like, "See you next time." It was as if they were condoning her behaviour and expecting it. That made me incredibly angry. I was desperate. I didn't know what to do about her. She'd get home and fall asleep. There were problems at school. This group had taken vodka onto the school premises. Nadia's life was in a downward spiral and I had no one to turn to.'

Nadia started being rude to her mother as well as hanging around with one boy whose family Meta was concerned about. 'Nadia started going out with the son of this family. It was a nightmare. Now Nadia was swearing at me and that was completely out of character. One night, I suspected she was staying at this house. I called the police and they refused to act. This was my 13-year-old daughter. I told them that I was going down there myself. I was raging by now. I was in such a state. The police did turn up in the end and followed me to the house. I knocked on the door. She was in there with her boyfriend, but they refused to come to the door. There was nothing I could do. The police didn't do anything. I had to leave her there. I just didn't know how to pull her out of this situation. It was a complete disaster.'

On 27 November 2001, just before Nadia's 14th birthday, the situation got completely out of hand. 'She'd actually settled down a bit at school,' says Meta. 'She was coming back for tea at 5pm, but this day was different. She went to school but she didn't come home.' By midnight, Meta was frantic. She phoned the police, but they didn't turn up until 4am. Obviously, they weren't taking her disappearance seriously because she'd done it so often before. When Nadia didn't turn up in the morning, Meta knew something was seriously wrong.

The next day Meta discovered that another girl had gone missing from school as well, but she didn't even recognise this girl's name because she was new there. 'That day, first of all, I was angry with her,' says Meta. 'I was thinking, how dare she do this? Then I was scared. I was imagining that someone could have killed her and she could be lying dead somewhere. It was terrible. I felt ill. My whole life came to a standstill. Everyone was out looking for her, including my daughter Samantha, but nobody had seen her. These girls had simply disappeared.'

Meta couldn't do anything or think of anything else. She couldn't even bear to go to the shops because people would ask about Nadia and she couldn't face that. 'People put posters up down on the front in Leigh-on-Sea,' she says, 'but I couldn't stop collapsing and crying. All my kids were helping out and, after a week, we went to Missing People. The police had already been informed and I expected them to get a report in the local paper but they didn't. I wasn't in my right mind. I was a mess.

ove: Kate and Gerry McCann attend a church service in Praia de Luz, Portugal, to
k the 100-day anniversary of the disappearance of their daughter Madeleine.

ow: The McCanns return to England. Their bravery in the light of such tragedy and
speculation has been remarkable.

Above: Handsome Eddie Gibson, who went missing in Cambodia.

Below: Jo, Eddie's mum, with him in Sydney during his gap year in 2004.

Above: Sharon and Mark Roberts on their wedding day.

Below: Renewing their vows in Wales in 2004.

Above: Rebecca Carr with her son, Tyler.
Below: Tyler with 'Grandpops', his great grandfather.

Above: Nicki Durbin is adamant that her son, Luke, did not run away from home.

Below left: Richard Daniel and his brother Darren with stepfather Roger and baby Rick. Richard is wearing the stripy shirt.

Below right: Graham, Richard Daniel's father, pictured top left.

Above: Nadia Belhaj (*left*), just before she disappeared.

Below: Nadia and her mum, Meta. Nadia is now happily reunited with her family.

e: Lee with mum Christine and sister Lindsay. He was fifteen when he disappeared
Christine hopes that he is out there somewhere.

w: Lee with his father, Peter.

Above left: Derek Burns was a happy baby; he is pictured with his parents and older brother Gordon.

Above right: At first Derek did well at secondary school, but after a while he started play truant from school.

Below: On the trip to Zimbabwe. Derek is pictured with his mum, Diane, in front of Victoria Falls.

Luckily, I had a dog, which I had to take for walks. It kept a sort of routine. But when I was on the walks, I'd imagine arms and legs sticking out of the bracken. It was horrific. My imagination was running riot.'

At least Meta could talk to the other girl's mother and know that they were going through the same awful experience together. 'We went and did an appeal on *GMTV*,' she says. 'We were interviewed by Fiona Phillips and Eamonn Holmes. I remember looking up at the screens and seeing all these huge images of Nadia everywhere. That was very strange. I felt completely collapsed inside. I have no idea how I got through that day.' People rang in and said they'd seen them, but nothing came of it.

Then one day, Samantha phoned and said a body had been found nearby. 'I nearly passed out,' said Meta. 'In my mind, I could see Nadia's body lying there on the beach.' To Meta's immense relief, it wasn't, but this all added to the enormous strain of having a young daughter who was missing.

The family then heard through Missing People that Nadia and her friend had been spotted in London's Old Kent Road. Meta's eldest daughter, Niki, went looking but didn't find them. 'Missing People were the only ones who really looked after us and the other family. They made us feel as though they were genuinely looking for our daughters,' says Meta. 'They phoned every day to tell me about any possible sightings and to ask how I was. I was annoyed with the police. They really didn't seem to be doing anything at all.'

Christmas 2006 came for the Belhaj family and it was simply horrendous. 'I tried to do some Christmas shopping but I couldn't bear people coming up to me and asking about Nadia.

It was too painful,' she says. 'I'd get onto the bus and be filled with panic and want to cry. I remember getting home, falling into the house and onto to the stairs in total despair. I was making noises like an animal in pain. I didn't know what to do with myself. My dog would come and nuzzle me and look after me. I felt so alone. My son, Tarik, was living with me, which helped, but I was only just surviving.'

On Christmas Day, the family met up as usual, but there was a lot of silence. The silence was the absence of words they didn't speak about Nadia. 'There was only Nadia to talk about but somehow we couldn't do it,' says Meta. 'Everyone was thinking maybe she's dead but no one dared voice it. I was preparing myself mentally for when the police came to the door and told me she was dead. What would I say? How was I going to act? Those were the questions I had constantly going through my head. On Christmas Eve, I'd even written a poem to her explaining how much I missed her.'

Boxing Day came and went. It was now 30 days since the girls had gone missing. The day after that, Meta went to bed about 1am. 'I'd been talking to the dog, saying things like, "Where do you think she is?" and she'd put her face on my face and be very loving, and then I drifted off. Suddenly, the phone went and it was Southend police saying simply that my daughter had been found. For a split second, when I realised it was the police, I imagined that they were going to tell me she was dead,' she says. 'But they said she was at the police station in Battersea and could I go and collect her.'

First of all, Meta couldn't speak, then she burst into tears. It was such a shock. Especially when she'd been preparing herself mentally for bad news. Eventually, she got Samantha to go to London with her. On the way, she was worrying what state Nadia would be in and about whether she would actually want to come home. As they walked into the police station, her eyes were immediately drawn to a figure that she knew was her daughter.

'She looked terrible. She'd obviously been sleeping rough,' says Meta. 'She'd lost weight, she was filthy and she stank. She came up to me and said, "Hello," as if we'd seen each other yesterday, then we hugged and cried and held onto one another. After that, we bundled both girls into a cab and I held onto both of them. Out of love and fear. I still didn't know if they wanted to be found. We dropped the other girl off at her mother's and I was finally going home with my daughter, who was very much alive. I was so relieved.'

At home, the dirty, exhausted Nadia fell into bed and slept and slept. 'She was so shattered,' says Meta. 'I went to bed but I couldn't sleep. I was worrying that she wouldn't be there in the morning. It took me a long time to relax around her being home. I thought she was going to run off again, but she didn't. This time she had come home to stay. I could start to be happy again.'

Nadia wouldn't talk to Meta about what she'd done during her 31 days missing from home but Meta gradually found out when her daughter did interviews. 'It made me really angry that she wouldn't talk about her time away, I needed to know,' says Meta, 'but I just had to accept it's what she wanted to do.'

Fed up with school, Nadia has claimed in magazine articles that her friend and herself had no specific plans to run away. 'We just got the train up to London, then wandered the streets,' she says. 'We didn't really think about it. But as soon as we'd done it, we had to stay away. We only had ten pence between us. At first it seemed like a big adventure. It felt good being away and nobody telling me what to do, but it didn't stay that way. The first night, we slept out by London Bridge with just a puffer jacket over us.'

The girls slept rough at least part of the time in a burned-out car off the Old Kent Road. They stole food to survive, and clothes, bunked buses and begged for money during the day. One day, a generous man gave her £20. Another man stole her gold chain after saying he was going to have it valued. 'Harsh reality did set in,' she says. 'I'd go to a public loo and look in the mirror, think, God, what are you doing? Then I'd curl up in a ball and cry. When I look back now, I'm horrified by what we did then, but it was the only way we could survive.'

Of course, they got hassled by men on the street. 'One night, some Albanians smuggled us into their hostel, only to demand sex in return,' she says, 'but we escaped through a window and down a drainpipe.' Now she realises what an incredibly lucky escape that was. 'Christmas Day was really awful,' she says. I remembered how our family always spent it with Mum. I missed home so much but I couldn't bring myself to call her. In fact, we did get taken in by a couple who fed us and let us use their shower. But when they went to bed, we stole some of their clothes. Everything was about survival.'

They were found because someone at a hostel recognised them from the Missing People poster and called the police. 'I didn't realise what I'd put my mum through,' she says. 'I put myself in so much danger. It's only afterwards that I realised how fortunate I was to return safely.'

Nadia returned to her family. She knew they were so lucky

not to have been raped and robbed during her time living rough on the streets, and she settled down. She had her own daughter, Chloe, when she was 15. Now 20, Nadia lives up the road from her mother and Chloe is 5. She is a loving mother and Meta is a proud grandmother. Sometimes, even now, Meta gets upset about Nadia running away. But she also gets gorgeous Mother's Day cards, which tell her in no uncertain terms just how much Nadia loves her.

Chapter Eight

I Found My Dad
30 Years Later

Richard Daniel was a bonny four-year-old when his entire universe was upset. Of course, he was too young to understand then that this single event was going to affect him for the next 30 years.

It was 1974 and, even in Welwyn Garden City in Hertfordshire, young men like Richard's good-looking father, 21-year-old Graham, had succumbed to rock'n'roll hairstyles that trailed over shirt collars. Dark-haired Graham played the saxophone and organ for a rock band in his spare time at the local working men's club.

The truth is this attractive bread-delivery man fancied himself as a rock star in waiting and, five years earlier, he had impressed jolie laide local girl Teresa at that very club. At 17 she became pregnant by him with Darren and at 19 she gave birth to their second son – smiling, sensitive Richard.

The couple married in their teens, having started their

coupledom in a caravan in Teresa's mum's garden. 'You've made your bed, now lie in it,' her mum stated grittily to her daughter.

Eventually, Graham and Teresa managed to rent a two-bedroom house next to the railway line of the up-and-coming new town. There was a thriving community in Welwyn Garden City and that was why they liked it. But there were already severe cracks in their relationship. It had been rocky from Teresa's first pregnancy, which had come way too early for the pair. They found themselves on a slippery slope as a couple and it only got worse after the birth of Richard.

One of their problems was that Graham was a man of the 1970s and he liked to be a bit of a free spirit. He was a passionate naturist, feeling that taking his clothes off made him free and part of a more relaxed society. Teresa had a strict upbringing from her stern Polish mother and she would never entertain the notion of public nudity. Her mother, Lena, had worked in the work camps in Poland during WWII and she was a stickler for privacy. Under her tutelage, her daughter was the same.

So the rows started and continued. For their young sons, this turbulence was the norm. Teresa and Graham would scream at each other during their argumants and the sensitive little boy was terrified and very upset by what he saw. He felt the house was filled with a feeling of pervasive, impending doom.

Graham, in a misguided attempt to keep his wife happy, asked his married but extrovert friend, Roger, to visit. He hoped Theresa would be entertained by his humour. Entrenched in an antagonistic relationship, she was entertained by much more. Lean, long haired and handsome, Roger was witty and attentive.

During one particularly volatile argument between Graham and Teresa, sparked by Teresa's growing closeness to Roger, they failed to notice that four-year-old Richard, an emotional little boy, was standing very, very still, petrified by the awful sight of his mother and father locked into a violent battle. This unbearable image still sears into Richard's psyche and, even after counselling, he isn't able to erase it.

Teresa and Graham's marriage didn't survive. In fact, it was at that point in 1974 that Richard's childhood world collapsed, never to be entirely rebuilt. Soon afterwards, Teresa took her sons and all their belongings and moved in with Roger.

The tragedy for Richard and his older brother, Darren, was that they were never to see their father again. Well, not for 30 years. He literally disappeared from their lives. That chapter of Teresa's life had ended and she conclusively slammed the door on it. She never mentioned Graham again – apart from a few insults that passed her lips, that was it. Graham turned into the family secret. Yet in young Richard's mind, Graham was alive, well and severely missed. His daddy had gone missing and nobody would talk about it. He suffered his lot silently because that's what everyone else seemed to be doing.

For the next 30 years, Richard's only hazy memory of his real father was of being driven around in Graham's blue van to gigs. Somehow, it was exciting – it was his dad as rock star and he carried this memory inside his head across three decades like a piece of buried treasure that sustained him in lonely times.

From the moment they moved in, Roger Daniel assumed the mantle of father. Now his two-bedroom house – which wasn't far from the old one in Welywn Garden City – was their new home, but to Richard it seemed strange and overwhelming. He was traumatised and he became quiet and withdrawn for a year. Roger's family would try to spoil him as the youngest, but Richard was so scared of this new-found attention that on one occasion he hid behind his mother and, horror of all horrors, he wet himself. He never forgot that early humiliation and, somehow, it ruined his relationship with his new family.

However, at least the new house had a bigger garden for the boys to play in. Roger was an active 'father' – he liked playing football with them. He was also more outgoing than Graham, a bit of a lad about town who knew lots of different people and would introduce the boys to them. Gradually, the brothers did warm to him. The rest of the family had been encouraging them to call Roger 'Dad'. Darren and Richard resisted for a year, but then it somehow seemed the right thing to do. They were at a petrol station, Roger was paying at the kiosk and the boys made a pact – now it was going to be OK to for them to call him 'Dad'.

They put their plan into action straightaway and Roger was obviously chuffed. They left the petrol station with an official new father. A year after they'd moved in, he had been promoted. But just because they were calling him 'Dad' didn't mean to say that Richard wasn't still thinking about his real dad – he was. But no one else knew about this secret activity.

A couple of years later, Roger and Teresa got married and he legally adopted the boys. They had to go to court and say they agreed to it. The building was intimidating, but they did get an ice cream treat in London afterwards. It was significant in that Richard and Darren now took on the surname Daniel. Their father's surname of Cole was removed. Roger's intentions were clearly honourable but merely resulted in reducing their real father even further in their lives.

Meanwhile, Teresa was working for the healthcare company Roche as a laboratory assistant and she was so focused on financial survival that she didn't observe her little boys' internal struggles. Then she got pregnant and gave birth to Mark, her third son. So they moved to another house, this time with three bedrooms. It was a definite improvement, but having a new brother was a bit of a shock to the brothers' systems. Especially for Richard. He was distinctly reluctant to relinquish his position as youngest son.

The new house was also in Welwyn Garden City, near Roger's mother, who treated the elder boys as if they were aliens. After all, they weren't her real grandchildren. But Mark was. So the others received no Chrismas presents. Naturally, this made for an unhealthy dose of sibling rivalry, which would have repercussions later on.

At junior school, Richard yearned for a 'proper' mother and father like all the other kids. He was even bullied for not having a real dad. Again, he became withdrawn. Inside, he was convinced that if his real dad had been around, he would be fine. He longed to be normal.

Roger was a milkman and, after a few years, he became friendly with a woman who was working on his milk round as part of her summer job. Teresa suspected that something inappropriate was going on and a vicious argument followed between Teresa and Roger.

Inevitably, Teresa and Roger split up. But they got back together again only for their relationship to go from bad to worse. That was the end of their marriage.

Teresa completely cut off any communication with Roger after that. He tried to contact the boys but to no avail. It was the boys who were suffering the most in this second separation. The boys didn't see Roger for a couple of years after that.

Theirs was now a single-parent household in which Teresa was working, so Richard did a lot of taking care of his little brother, Mark. He sacrificed many of his early teenage years in order to be responsible for his younger brother. As a result, he turned into a bitter, angry youth. He even resented the younger boy for not being his full-brother. There was so much confusion and rejection in his life that he started to spurn his seven-year-old brother.

Richard was rapidly turning into a troubled young man. He hit walls and doors with his fists and he hung out with other disenfranchised young people with similar backgrounds. At 13, he was drinking alcohol, sniffing glue and smoking cannabis. Anything that could keep the pain of his missing father from hurting him was imbibed or smoked.

He was allowed out when Teresa arrived home after work so he'd stay out until 1am. Teresa hadn't the energy to do anything about it – she was a working, single mum with three boys at home, although Darren was, by this time, an independent 15-year-old. At one point, Teresa was so worn out by her existence that she went to stay with a woman friend.

Darren actually contacted Roger at that point, who moved back in for a couple of nights and helped them out with money. Meanwhile, Richard stuck to his routine of delivering Mark to school by bike. He was determined that the brothers would stick together and survive. They did.

During this period, Richard discovered one person that he

could talk to about his real dad: his nan, Lena – Teresa's mother. Lena had always liked Graham and she described him as a kind and loving man. Richard lapped up this information and tried to get her to tell him stories about his dad. He even started to imagine that one day he might meet him again.

At home, Richard would watch episodes of *Surprise, Surprise* on TV and fantasise that he would go on there himself and that Cilla Black would find his father for him. His favourite song during this period was 'Papa was a Rolling Stone' by the Temptations – he still loved to think of his father as a rock star. This was, of course, all going on in secret. Not a word was breathed to his brothers or his mother about it. Only his nan heard about his real thoughts because she encouraged them. Richard used to go round to visit her on his own when she moved to a flat nearby after her divorce. He savoured these intimate conversations with her. He felt seen and acknowledged for once. And gradually he began to think that meeting his father again would be possible one day.

His nan had started talking about the Salvation Army's tracing system. She'd even gone along and collected the forms for it. Richard began quietly to get excited. Inside. But his hopes were not to last. Just as he was becoming optimistic about the possibility of finding his dad, his nan had a massive heart attack and died at the age of 58. With her death, Richard gave up all of his hopes of seeing his father again. His nan had represented an important link to his real father and also a pragmatic support in looking for him. Now that all drained away.

Despair took over his adolescent body. His nan had promised that when they found Graham, she would come with him.

Now Richard felt bereft and totally daunted by the prospect of searching for his dad alone. His brother didn't seem to be interested. Instead, he looked for hedonistic ways of assuaging his pain.

At 17, Richard was taking speed, ecstasy and LSD. Reality wasn't something he wanted to confront. It was way too painful so he found ways of escaping it. He worked with Darren putting in double glazing by day and found drugs at night. The job didn't last because he became too erratic. Unable to see any light at the end of his tunnel in the search for his father, he pushed the self-destruct button. Big time.

Richard ended up without a home. He moved into a flat with his brother, Darren, then he moved back in with his mother, who had remarried. But she had house rules that didn't suit him – he wasn't allowed to have friends round. Richard was far too disturbed and out of it to last long in that environment. His stay only lasted a few weeks.

Anyway, now he had a new family – it was the acid-house era in 1989 and his mates were all taking ecstasy. The touchy-feely world of ecstasy opened up to him and embraced him. At last, Richard felt close to other people, albeit after several ecstasy pills. He even found his first girlfriend, Sherry. It was perfect. He could take ecstasy with her and they could escape awful reality together. All his friends were from single-parent families, or adopted, or from some sort of harsh background, because he couldn't actually bear to have friends who had two parents. That's how bad it was. He couldn't relate to them and his damaged psyche would have gone into overload if he'd got anywhere near them.

He also started a pattern of behaviour that was to persist

in his relationships with women over the years. The 19-year-old Sherry told him that her father had abused her — naturally this triggered Richard's sense of moral outrage and he went into the role of rescuer and protector. It turned out that Sherry wasn't telling the truth. Richard was looking after his girlfriend's needs when he actually needed to look after his own. It was classic co-dependent behaviour. They spent three years together, but in the end Richard couldn't handle his role of permanent protector. Even with the help of ecstasy.

Next, he found himself being attracted to Jackie, who — wait for it — had a couple of children and a violent ex-partner, and an even bigger need for his protection. Richard was in and out of jobs, taking huge amounts of class-A drugs, drinking too much and trying desperately to help Jackie out. Sometimes, she would just sit in a corner, rocking. He would go over and hold her. It was a relationship that was doomed to failure.

Richard was avoiding his own damage — and his search for his missing dad — by involving himself in Jackie's difficult life. Big hearted as he was, he introduced her to lots of his friends and supported her when she gave up one of her children for adoption. But it all blew up in his face. When she got stronger, she no longer wanted him around. She dumped him and chucked him out.

Now he was homeless in a more serious way. He was 25, without hope and homeless. He spent the next couple of years on friends' sofas. He even ended up in the bin cupboards of various blocks of flats in the neighbourhood. But mostly he was sofa-surfing. He would do a nightshift cleaning and they would do a dayshift. He'd sleep on the sofa during the day while they were out. Sometimes, he even dealt ecstasy to his friends in order to make extra cash.

He soon found another girlfriend called Sarah, who had two kids as well. But he didn't want to move in with her. He was becoming wary. One day, he lost his job and fell out with a friend – it was too much. He took some LSD, which was, of course, distinctly unwise. It took him right over the edge into madness. He no longer wanted to live.

He found himself covered in blood in a pub toilet. He'd punched the drying machine so hard that his hands were badly cut up. Suicide seemed like the best option at this point in his troubled life. Richard had had enough of the traumas that the universe had put in his path. He craved peace, far away from all this chaos and rejection. He wanted out, then and there.

Amazingly, his younger brother, Mark, happened to be in the pub and managed to help Richard. There was no more sibling rivalry between them – now they supported one another. Mark rang his dad to ask if Richard could come to stay with them. Mark was to become something of a saviour for his elder brother. He was a rarity – someone that Richard could depend on in times of adversity. Richard moved in with his stepdad and stepbrother for a couple of years. It was a brief period of stability for him.

He even started thinking about his real dad again and imagined a future meeting with him. Occasionally, Roger would say something derogatory about Graham being a naturist but Richard was too upset to actually voice his support of his dad.

Not long afterwards, at a cousin's 21st-birthday celebration, Richard's older brother, Darren, finally broke down about their dad. In the middle of the festivities and after a few drinks, Darren started crying, which was totally out of character. 'We've got to find our real dad,' he declared. Richard was shocked that his brother felt this way. He had thought he was alone in such feelings of loss and yearning. But now he had found an ally in his brother.

This declaration from Darren changed Richard's perspective yet again. Now he understood that both he and his brother wanted to find their real dad, the world looked different – now everything seemed possible. It was an epiphany for Richard. He stopped doing drugs and put his life back together again. He even started a college course in landscape gardening. Sadly, just as he was relaxing into this brand-new existence, stepdad Roger found a new partner and he had to move out. Back into the vicious circle.

Poor Richard was homeless yet again. He moved in with his girlfriend, Sarah, who, in an echo of Richard's search, had recently contacted her own real mother in Zimbabwe but it hadn't worked out. They met but they tragically didn't get on. Sarah was distraught at this second loss of her mother as she'd invested so much in the fantasy of being in contact with her. The realisation that it wasn't going to work knocked her for six. She spiralled into depression. Richard was, naturally, deeply affected by her disappointment and absorbed the information that he, too, could be let down in a reunion with his own dad. Sarah's news terrified him and put him off searching for a while. The couple soon split up.

Homeless yet again, Richard had another blow. He'd actually garnered enough points with the council for his own flat but, because of his constant moving, he'd missed the letter telling him about it. The council cancelled his points and announced he'd have to start again. He was understandably distraught at this news. It literally felt as though the heavens were against him. He started to seriously think about suicide again. He actually went out and bought some rope. He was planning to hang himself outside the council building. He was becoming more and more anxious, depressed and out of touch with reality.

Fortunately, yet again, Mark phoned him and worked out what was going on. Again the rescuer went into action. He organised for his older brother to go up to their mother's in Northamptonshire, where she was living with her third husband, Steve. Richard went but didn't like it there. He only lasted a few weeks. He didn't like Steve – he wanted his real dad.

The thought, Why can't I have a normal mum and dad who live together? was still a regular visitor to Richard's beleaguered mind. By this time, Teresa had started to realise that not having any contact with his real dad had seriously affected Richard's mental health and she tried to make up for the past by reaching out to him. But Richard, now in his late-20s and broken, couldn't accept her kindness – he simply didn't trust her.

A tiny ray of sunshine broke through the carapace of Richard's troubled life at this stage. A second cousin was found in Bedford, who worked for a hostel for the homeless. She managed to get Richard a room. It was next to the toilet and grimly decorated, but this step into his own space marked the beginning of his recovery.

He was referred to a psychiatrist, diagnosed with depression and was prescribed medication. He also received counselling, which helped him recognise the different types of patterns that controlled his life in a negative way. He began an important journey of self-awareness while living among heroin addicts and alcoholics.

There was a lovely Welsh man called Ralph who worked in the dingy hostel. Richard was able to open up to him because he seemed so utterly caring. He told him how much he'd wanted to commit suicide, and all about his childhood history. Ralph came up with a simple solution. 'Why don't you find your dad?' he asked. 'You've lost so much, things can only get better.'

At first, Richard refused to consider this course of action openly, even though he'd been thinking about it inside for 30 years. He was so terrified of rejection and failure. But one day, he decided to ask his brother, Mark, if he would mind if he looked for his real dad. After all, Graham wasn't Mark's dad and Richard, ever a sensitive soul, didn't want to upset the younger brother who had come to his rescue so often. Mark said he was fine with it. Richard consulted Darren, who was positively over the moon. 'We've got to find him now,' he said, his voice pumping with excitement.

They started by asking their mother to give them information. She didn't know much. She knew the name of Graham mother's and where he used to work — that was it. Good old Ralph at the hostel helped Richard contact the Salvation Army. Richard was almost overwhelmed by the questions on the form they sent him. He could hardly bear the emotions he had simply by reading them. One was, 'Why do you want to find your relative?' That threw him completely. In the end, he settled for a neutral-sounding 'For medical reasons'. What he wanted to write was 'Because I've missed and needed him for the last 30 years'.

Richard was scared of the ramifications of filling in this form – that he might actually trace his real dad – to the extent that he had to persuade his brother, Darren, to come down and watch him post the envelope. The act of posting it with Darren watching seemed to make it a part of some ritual for finding their dad. Not a rain dance to invoke the rain, but a dad ritual to invoke the discovery of their dad. It was such a significant, emotional event that they had both to be there to wish the form well on its journey. All their hopes and dreams were in that envelope.

A week later, Richard settled into the non-threatening idea that nothing was going to happen; that he'd never hear from the Salvation Army again. He was almost creating defeat with his mental attitude. Another two weeks went by and then it happened. Out of the blue. The Salvation Army rang up with momentous news. In fact, it was more than momentous – it was amazing, unbelievable news. 'Your dad is going to phone you in fifteen minutes,' said the woman on the end of the phone.

Richard entered into a surreal zone of non-belief as adrenaline started to pump around his body. The next 15 minutes were the scariest in Richard's life. He hadn't spoken to his real father for 30 years, although he'd thought about doing so constantly – and now it was going to happen. Just like that. No letters exchanged first. He'd imagined it would be a long process, which would allow him to get used to the idea inside himself first. This immediacy stunned and frightened him.

He telephoned Darren, who was equally shocked. Richard was so scared the reality of his father wouldn't live up to his dreams that he contemplated turning his mobile off. The butterflies were screaming in his belly. He didn't want to face the very real emotions that he might have to feel. Sadness, loss, excitement, possible rejection, failure and anticipation all merged into one big blur of feelings.

The phone rang. A stranger's voice said incredulously, 'You're my son.' His father couldn't hold back the tears. Thirty years of not seeing or talking to his sons gushed out. He couldn't help himself. Richard was in a state of shock.

'Don't cry,' he just about managed to say while holding back his own tears. The call didn't last long, but it was long enough for Richard to realise that his dad did want to see him again. Hallelujah! It was true, if unbelievable. His dad wanted to see him and his brother just as much as they wanted to see him. They arranged to meet up at Darren's flat a week later.

Meanwhile, always thinking of others, Richard phoned his other brother. Mark's response was more guarded this time. He could obviously sense a change in the family set-up on the horizon and he wasn't sure about it. He also asked the challenging question, 'Why didn't Graham try to find you?' He was trying to protect Richard, not wanting to see him hurt by further rejection. He didn't want to have to rescue him from another attempt at suicide.

For the next seven days, Richard slept fitfully and fretfully, allowing to surface in his mind all the questions to which he had ever wanted to know the answer. What was his dad like now? Would they like each other? Would he really want to have a relationship with his sons? Would he disappear again afterwards? Would they be like him in any way? Would the meeting be a success? Did his dad have a wife now? Or any other children? The questions wouldn't stop coming.

A week later, as Richard climbed the stairs of Darren's maisonette flat, drops of sweat were pouring down his neck. He was terrified of this encounter with his father – after all, he'd imagined it for so long and it might go horribly wrong. Darren was nervous as well, so nervous he ended up fleeing the flat in search of milk to escape the initial encounter. 'You can't leave me, you bastard!' pleaded Richard. But Darren went anyway. Emotions do funny things to people.

Alone, Richard stared out of the window. It was as though time was standing still and he was inside a painting of himself. He realised that a silver-coloured Sierra had driven up. A man in a baseball cap got out and was coming to the door. Richard held his breath, pure fear and elation mixed together. He opened the door and there stood his dad, his real dad, looking funnily enough just like Who guitarist Pete Townshend.

Thirty years of longing hit his chest. His heart was almost exploding as he hugged that intimate stranger. Graham was crying copiously. He was crying for all the missing hours, days, nights, months and years that they had been apart. He couldn't hold back this river of tears and he didn't want to. Richard just looked at him in pure shock and amazement.

Finally, they sat down on the sofa. Probably because he was so nervous, Graham ended up blurting out that he was still a naturist. It was such a ridiculous piece of information that both of them burst into spontaneous laughter. In fact, they couldn't stop laughing – this was their incredulity at what was happening. And their joy. And the release of all those pent-up difficult emotions that they'd kept locked inside for all these years.

Darren eventually made it back with the milk. There was

another hug and more father and son acknowledgement. For the next hour and a half, they talked and laughed. Graham also told them he had a partner and a daughter called Emma, and another son called Richard. This information made Richard feel a little strange. But later he decided it was a good sign. That, in fact, Graham had been in some way remembering him by also calling his other son Richard.

After this first meeting, Richard was gradually able to erase his childhood image of his dad. Now at last he could form his own independent view of his real father. He could finally discard his mother's words and decide himself. That was a huge liberation for him. There was also his new extended family to think about. Not just a brother and sister but a niece called Maya as well. Darren and Richard were uncles. At last, he could feel that his life was changing for the better and a surge of new warmth filled his heart.

But it wasn't straightforward. He was hopeful but also fearful of having a half-sister. He knew he didn't relate to women very well, so he was worried about meeting Emma. But he needn't have been so scared. They all met up the following week. Emma's bubbly nature took care of Richard's quietness. As he'd found on first meeting his real dad, the words they exchanged weren't profound – they talked about the mundane details of their daily lives – but the meeting was. This was the beginning of a new family life for Richard and it was to make a fundamental difference to how he saw the world.

Despite the years apart, amazingly Darren shared characteristics with Graham. They both said 'Sorry' all the time and stuttered when they were nervous. The shared genetics were clear to see. For Richard, there was the comfort of knowing that he had a real dad who wanted to know him that brought real healing.

Five years later, they are still building memories and creating a close relationship. Graham has even given up being a naturist. He said he was bored with it and has taken up reiki instead. He even uses it on his sons when they have aching necks – it's all part of getting to know and love each other; all part of their not-so-new, treasured relationship.

'It feels as though I've known him all my life,' says Richard with a smile that doesn't need explanation. After 30 years, Richard has really found his father and his own *raison d'etre*. What's more, his dad did look like a rock star.

Chapter Nine

We've Never Stopped Waiting For You to Walk In

Lee Boxell's bedroom is frozen in time. There are fading posters of Mel and Kim, Sam Fox and T'Pau's Carol Decker, all pop queens in 1988. There are football posters from his favourite local team, Sutton United, which are coming unstuck from the wall. There is a wardrobe full of the then 15-year-old teenager's clothes. There's even his aftershave, Insignia, hiding in one of the drawers. Nothing has changed since 10 September 1988. That was when Lee disappeared.

His mother, Christine Boxell, reacted to the boy's disappearance by not wanting to change his blue bedroom one iota. Some people think this means she hasn't moved on. But she is clear that she wants Lee's bedroom to remain faithful to the day that he went out and never returned. 'I suppose it is like a shrine to him,' she says, 'but I hope one day he will come back and I want everything to be exactly the same as when he left. There are all his records and his hi-fi too. I couldn't go in his bedroom for a very long time after Lee went missing, but now I've made it my office. I do my market research there. Sometimes, I'll smell his aftershave and to me it's as though he is there with me.'

Lee's parents, now in their 60s, and his 31-year-old sister, Lindsay, have had the awful challenge of having to live for the last 19 years without knowing what happened to Lee. Fortunately, they are a very close family so they have closed ranks and supported one another as much as they can from the intrusion of the outside world. They've been terribly brave in the face of ineffable sadness and a distressing lack of information about Lee's whereabouts.

The Boxells are an average middle-class family who live in Sutton, Surrey. Peter Boxell is an architect, Christine volunteers at the local hospital and helps her neighbours. Lee was their first child. 'We had a nice three-bedroom house. I was twenty-nine,' says Christine. 'We planned to have a baby and he arrived in 1972. He was a grand little baby, although it was a difficult birth and he was put into special care for a while afterwards. He was a placid baby.'

By the time Lee was seven, the Boxells had moved to Hanover in Germany, where Peter was designing military buildings on a three-year contract. 'The children went to a British military school,' she says, 'and it was a great life being with the army. Everyone was in the same boat and we all pulled together. There were lots of different activities for the families and children. It was wonderful. But I did miss my family and my mother was ill. Then my sister had cancer so it was problematic for me in that way. We made the most of being in Europe though. We bought a caravan and toured Italy and France in our holidays.'

When Lee was ten and Lindsay was seven, they came back to live in Sutton. 'Lee saw all his old friends again,' says Christine. 'We were all happy to be back. At ten, Lee's teeth started to stick out and that was a bit of a problem for him. He didn't say he was bullied but I'm sure it was hard for him. I took him to an orthodontist, which he didn't like but, a couple of years later, his teeth were perfect again and he'd grown into a good-looking boy.'

Christine mentions that Lee was a little slow in a few areas of learning. 'He couldn't catch a ball for a long time,' she says. 'He was quite immature for his age. At school, he plodded along but he was never really academic.' Instead, Lee was kind, just like his mother. He would go out of his way to help other people. 'If he saw an old lady trying to cross the road, he would go over and give her a hand,' says Christine. 'I help at a club for the elderly and he'd come along and hoover for me. He was lovely like that.'

Teenage Lee was not a streetwise boy. 'When he learned to play football, he was always outside our house on the green with his friends kicking a ball around,' says Christine. 'But he still used to go out with us a lot. He wasn't independent.'

As for girlfriends, he hadn't yet got to that stage. 'I'm sure he would have loved a girlfriend,' says his mother, 'but he didn't yet have that kind of confidence. Carol Decker from T'Pau was his favourite in the pop world and he did take a neighbour's daughter to Capital Radio concert, but I think I asked her for him.'

In the summer of his Year Ten at school, Lee did work experience at Barclays Bank in Cheam. 'He made himself indispensable,' says Christine. 'He made the tea, he took out the rubbish. He would do anything and everything. They really liked him there and even offered him a job when he left school. He was very proud of that.'

Lee had always said that he wanted to join the police force. 'He would get me to measure him periodically,' says Christine, 'to see if he'd grown enough. At that time, you had to be five feet, eight inches to join and, the last time I measured him, he was five feet, six inches. He was excited because he was almost tall enough.'

He was also an avid Sutton United fan. He used to go to their matches up the road with neighbourhood friends, Anthony and Russell. 'His dad was never a football fan,' says Christine, 'but Lee loved football. I bought him the blue-and-white scarf and hat. He used to hide them under his coat, then put them on when he got to the grounds.'

By the age of 15, Lee was a happy-go-lucky but slightly naive boy. He loved pop quizzes and football. In September 1988, he'd just started back at school after the summer holidays. Christine recalls that he was pleased because he'd paid the money for some of extra school books before anyone else in his class.

On 9 September 1988, Lee was round at Russell's house nearby and they discussed going to a football match the next day. 'Sutton United were playing in Blackpool so Lee wasn't going to that match because it was too far away,' she says, 'and they were thinking about going to Wimbledon or Selhurst Park. My mother was very ill so I was thinking of going to see her that Saturday.'

The following morning, Saturday, Lee was lounging around downstairs in his pajamas, being a bit grumpy in a teenage kind of way. 'I asked what he was going to do and he said he was going to a football match, but they were going to decide later,' she says. 'I was eager to go to my mother's and I didn't drive then, so I had to get the bus. The plan was for us all to meet there in the evening and I would cook everyone a meal.' Christine left with a simple goodbye and she has not seen Lee since.

But in every other way it was an ordinary day in the Boxell household. Christine had gone to see her sick mother. Peter gave Lindsay a lift to her friend's house and then came back and painted the back fence. Lee went off to meet Russell and do some shopping in Sutton. He only had £10 on him.

The boys called in on Russell's mother, Joan, who worked in a newspaper shop in Sutton. She asked them where they were going and they still didn't know. Then Russell made an unexpected decision. He changed his mind and said he was going home to watch the horse-racing with his father. Now Lee was left to decide what he was going to do and, fatefully, he made up his mind to go to a football match on his own. Nobody even knows which match he'd decided to go to. The last sightings of Lee were of him going to towards Sutton train station. Of course, in those days there were no CCTV cameras.

That day, Charlton Athletic were playing Millwall at Selhurst Park. Christine thinks it's very unlikely that Lee would have gone on his own to this match because the Millwall fans had a bad reputation and Lee would have been frightened. On the other hand, Selhurst Park is nearby, so it remains a possibility. Otherwise, he would have made his way to Wimbledon. The trouble is nobody knows what Lee did. They only know he did not come home and that was utterly devastating for his family.

He could have got on a train and got lost. He could have gone to Wimbledon. He could have met up with someone who persuaded him to go with them. 'He was a very trusting boy and very naive,' says Christine. 'He might have gone off with someone if they'd told him they had tickets for a match. Lee wasn't suspicious enough about people.'

Christine was at her mother's, helping out without a worry in her head. She thought she knew that Lee was with Russell at a football match. She phoned home at 5pm and Lee wasn't there, but that was normal – it was too early for him to be back. But when she rang at 6pm and he still wasn't there, she did start worrying. The welcome news didn't come. The hours passed and she was still ringing home but there was no sign of Lee.

'By 10pm, I was frantic because I knew Lee would have rung home,' she says. 'He would have been scared to have been out so late. Peter was a bit more laid back at first; he was trying to allay my fears. He said that he thought Lee was probably with his friend, Anthony, and that they would turn up soon. In my mind, I knew something was wrong. I was still at my mother's but I decided I had to get home.'

Christine is not even sure how she got home, but she assumes she called a taxi and arrived at about 12am. 'That's when we rang the police,' she says, 'but they didn't take us seriously. They noted that "Lee Boxell, fifteen" was missing but that was it. They assumed that he'd run away. The police weren't very good at handling this kind of missing case in those days. That was very frustrating for me. I knew how out of character it was for Lee to disappear. I knew he would never run away, but the police didn't take any notice of my opinion.'

Peter and Christine also rang all the hospitals. He wasn't

there. At 2am, they heard Anthony come home with his parents and they hoped desperately that Lee was with them. They managed to convince each other that he was. He wasn't. A policeman came round the following morning and took a statement. 'I just wanted the police to get out there and look for Lee,' she says. 'I think they did take Peter out in one of the police cars around the streets of Sutton but he wasn't found.'

Christine went into shock. She couldn't comprehend what was going on. She certainly couldn't accept that her lovely Lee was missing and they didn't know where he was. 'I did everything I could think of to do,' she says. 'I ran round all the neighbours and asked them if they'd seen Lee. I was out of my mind with worry for several months. I wasn't eating. I was having terrible nightmares.'

Next, they had to go through the indignity of the forensic team going through their house looking for drugs or evidence of any physical conflict. 'We were under suspicion first of all,' she says, 'which again was hard, because I knew they were looking in the wrong place. I just wanted everyone to be out on the streets looking for my son.'

But by Monday, the police had gone into action. 'Now they had twenty-six officers on the case and a mobile unit. They were going on the trains saying, "Have you seen this boy?"' she says. 'But nobody had seen Lee. They had sniffer dogs out and they were searching the river but they found nothing at all. It was so frustrating and painful. I always wanted so much more to be done. I just wanted to have my Lee back.'

After a month, one of the detectives came round and informed Christine that, sadly, they had to take most of their officers off the case because they were needed elsewhere. 'It was a knockback,' she says, 'because the idea of them giving up sent me into panic. I remember saying to him that I would never give up looking for my son.' And she never has.

She kept herself busy with activities that were connected to Lee. 'I contacted Carol Decker from T'Pau and she took posters to her gigs,' says Christine. 'Selhurst Park, the football ground, put up posters of Lee, but we still didn't hear anything.'

At home, the family were dealing in different ways with Lee being missing. Peter internalised his feelings and didn't talk very much about what was going on, except in a practical way. 'Lindsay was only thirteen and she's a quiet person,' says Christine, 'so she didn't say much. Now I feel like I pushed Lindsay away during that time because I was so focused on looking for Lee. I feel guilty now. Later, she didn't even tell new friends that she had a brother. That was just her way of dealing with it.'

Christine, meanwhile, has never stopped talking about Lee, to friends and to the media in whatever way she can. 'It helps me to talk about him,' she says. 'It keeps him alive for me. For the first few months, I couldn't sleep or eat. I was imagining Lee lying somewhere, dead. I couldn't stop imagining possible scenarios.'

Lee went missing in the same year as Suzy Lamplugh. 'Her mother set up the Suzy Lamplugh Trust, then her friend, Mary Asprey, and her sister, Janet Newman, created the National Missing Persons Helpline,' says Christine. 'That's how it started.' Lee Boxell was the first missing person on their files.

Christine tried the Salvation Army but they didn't deal with missing persons under the age of 17. 'I didn't know where to go for help and support,' she says. 'There was so much less around then. I felt very alone with it all. But the people at the charity Missing People did a lot. I went on *Crimewatch* through them and did interviews in the newspapers. I went on *Kilroy*, which was good because I met other parents in the same position as me.'

Sharing stories and keeping in touch with parents in a similar position has helped Christine a lot. 'We talked on the telephone and still send each other cards at difficult times of the year like Christmas, or the birthdays of our children,' she says. 'That was very useful and meant I didn't feel so on my own with my emotions. Not knowing where your son is continues to be a terrible place to occupy emotionally. Talking to other people in the same position does help.'

Christine maintains the position mentally that she must remain hopeful. 'I have to be optimistic or else what else do I have?' she says. 'I don't want my head to be full of images of Lee somewhere, dead. That's too hard to bear. Obviously, I think it from time to time, but I try not to.' The whole family went on a programme in Holland, which was the equivalent of *Surprise, Surprise*. 'They had us on because the charity Missing People had found a missing Dutch person. It was sad for us though. Other people were being reunited with their families and I thought, somewhere in my mind, that perhaps they'd invited us on the programme because Lee had turned up.' But he hadn't.

Clairvoyants were another source of comfort and distraction for Christine. 'I must have seen more than a hundred over the years, ' she says, 'but it's very confusing because they all say different things. I didn't ever pay a penny but nothing concrete was ever established through them.' Seeing them, however, did provide a source of reassurance at times while, at others, it was also disturbing. One clairvoyant saw Lee lying on the railway track so they had the electricity to the tracks turned off to look for him.

'I don't think the police like clairvoyants much because they involve a lot of wrong leads, which wastes time,' says Christine. Another clairvoyant saw Lee in an alleyway in Carshalton. 'We went hunting for him there but we didn't find anything,' she says.

A radio clairvoyant demanded to see Lee's photograph but then announced he had bad news and asked if they wanted to hear it. 'He said Lee was dead and was somewhere in a twenty-mile radius of Sutton,' she says, 'which wasn't much use really. I was so upset by that information, I ran out of the house crying. I think the police told him off for that.'

The late psychic, Betty Shine, wrote Christine a letter saying that Lee had joined the army and gone abroad. 'There were so many stories and they were all different,' she says. 'It made me quite disillusioned. Peter said not to bother any more because they were all rubbish.'

Christine was once in a chapel in Richmond with a spiritual healer leading the service. 'We were singing hymns,' she says. 'Then this woman came up to me. She asked if I'd had a cream cake before I came, and I had. That was a bit weird, although Peter maintained I had some crumbs on my face. She then said she heard loud music and I started to cry because I thought that it was Lee. This woman promptly stopped talking to me. She said she couldn't do it if I was crying because tears send the spirits away. I think that said more about her than anything else.'

Another woman who'd heard about Lee disappearing came to their door with a bunch of flowers. 'She said she did clairvoyant work for the police, she wanted to help and she had got in touch with a spirit called John,' says Christine. 'There were so many different psychics.' There were the strange three ladies who turned up and said they wanted to go into Lee's room. 'They went up there and started screaming,' she recalls. 'They were in there all holding their throats. They said Lee had been strangled. That was too much. I had to get my friend to tell them to go.'

She even had a male nurse contact here and tell her he'd treated Lee in hospital. 'I wanted to tape our conversation but he freaked out,' she says. 'I asked him about any distinguishing marks that he'd noticed on Lee. It turned out this nurse was a drug addict. I really got all sorts getting in touch with me and I had to weed out the mad ones.'

Sadly, she hasn't seen Russell and his family for years now. It was difficult. The fact that Russell was the last to see her son and also that he made the decision to leave him and go home to be with his father has made Christine feel that Russell let her son down on a subconscious level. She's not the blaming type, but she can't help feeling life would have been so different if they'd stayed together that day.

Lee's other friend, Anthony, and his family have been endlessly supportive. 'We see each other a lot,' she says, 'and they always send a card on the anniversary of Lee going missing. I also think that an anonymous £1,000 reward was put up in 1988 by Anthony's dad. They're very kind and that's helped a lot.'

However, Anthony is 34 now and it is tough for Christine to keep in touch with him. 'Seeing him reminds me how old Lee is now,' she says. 'And it also reminds me of all the time we have lost between us. It is painful to see him because then I realise just how many years have passed since that afternoon in September 1988.'

Christine has also had to contend with her sister dying from cancer and mother dying from old age. 'It was hard saying goodbye to them both,' she says. 'But at least I could say goodbye. With Lee, it's unbearable because I've never been able to say goodbye. I've only got my niece left, but she has been incredibly supportive all these years. She's always there for me.'

Various police officers have come and gone. 'There was one detective who had left the force and decided to write a book,' she says. 'He came round and started telling me about what the police had done wrong in the original days of the case. That was upsetting and not a positive move.' In 2006, Missing People reopened Lee's case to try and find some new leads. They're looking at all the information from a different perspective. 'I liked it because it felt as though there was a focus on Lee again.'

Another time, a detective came and showed her a photo of a man in prison who said he'd been in love with a boy called Lee and had lived around the corner from their house. 'That was awful,' she says. 'I didn't recognise him but the police were going through his garage before the house was sold. It was traumatic to imagine what they might find but, in the end, they didn't find anything.'

For 19 years, the Boxell family have survived without knowing what has happened to their beloved son. To outsiders, it's unimaginable how they have got through. 'I do voluntary work at the hospital, which I love,' says Christine. 'I like chatting to all the patients and now I work in the shop there selling sweets. That really keeps me going. Plus I do market-research work and help out old-age pensioners by taking them out to afternoon clubs.'

Her daughter, Lindsay, recently got married and is now pregnant. 'The wedding was lovely,' says Christine. 'And it's great to have something optimistic to look forward to like a new baby in the family. I just have to be careful not to worry too much that something will go wrong. But it is fantastic that she's found a really nice husband and has settled down.'

There are dates in the year that are painful. There is Christmas and Lee's birthday, and the anniversary of the day he went missing. 'We don't open champagne at Christmas – it wouldn't feel right,' she says. 'I light a candle in a church and say my prayers, which are all about hoping Lee is out there somewhere still.'

People tell Christine that she's always laughing. 'But they don't realise what is going on inside me,' she says. 'In my heart, I'm devastated and I always will be until Lee turns up.

'We were just away on holiday and I started looking for him – but I'm still looking for a fifteen-year-old, not the thirty-four-year-old that he is today. So I do still have mad moments.' This anguish lies just beneath the surface and the only way Christine can deal with it is to focus on the hope that Lee is still alive.

Chapter Ten

My Big Brother Is Out There Somewhere, Living Like a Saint

Filmmaker Fred Scott is very close to his 35-year-old brother, Nicholas. They used to talk theology together when Nicholas was a student, and 28-year-old Fred has been on numerous missions to bring his elder brother home from places like Scotland and Bosnia. They would often embark on mini-adventures together. Nicholas went missing quite often, but he would always get in touch, usually when he didn't have any money and was starving.

All that changed on 15 July 2003. That was when Nicholas went missing from his home in Wandsworth and his family have not seen him again since. There was one early clue to his whereabouts – he withdrew £150 from a cash dispenser in Ancona, Italy, on 21 July. He has not been in contact and there have been no more withdrawals from his bank account. Four years later, he is still missing.

The Scotts are a resoundingly British, middle-class family.

Tim Scott used to be a major in the army while his wife, Susan, is one of those loving, stalwart mothers who is glamorous as well as being the backbone of the family. Nicholas was born in 1971, only 15 months after sister Catherine and the siblings went on to be very close.

'When we were little, we lived in a five-bedroom house on the edge of Dartmoor,' she says. 'Dad was in the army and spent a huge amount of time away. Nicholas and I were never apart. Whether it was learning to ride a bike or a small pony, being up to our knees in the little stream that flowed from the moors or huddled together in our wigwam with sweets from the local post office.'

Blond with lovely blue eyes, Nicholas adored his mother. While their father was away, it would be Nicholas who looked after her. He was a sweet little boy, always concerned about other people. The family decamped to Italy when Nicholas was six, while Tim studied at the NATO Defence College in Rome. They even met the Pope. The family's third child, Fred, was born when they moved to Dorset.

'I always looked up to Nicholas,' Fred says. 'He was always a good brother but it was always Nicholas and Catherine together and I'd be trying to be near them or do what they were doing.' Always on the move because of their father's job, they found themselves in a big house in Somerset in 1982, when third brother Peter was born.

In the meantime, Nicholas had become a boarder at a prep school near Swanage. However, Nicholas got a lot of comments about his size. He was small and the other kids wouldn't let him forget it.

'When he was eleven, he still looked eight,' says Catherine, 'and he became a target for some of the older boys. Late one night, he was even accosted by one of the other boys and sexually abused.' Sadly for him, he told the other boys the next day and then this humiliating news became the talk of the school. The boy who attacked him was quietly asked to leave the school but the sexual abuse continued to haunt Nicholas.

In an age and at a school that was less aware of the psychological effects of such abuse, Nicholas didn't get any help. In fact, he was still taunted for years afterwards by other boys who moved schools with him in Dorset. The impact of this sexual abuse is likely to have contributed to his psychological fragility later on. 'On one occasion when describing it and the impact it had had on him,' says Catherine, 'he cried and I felt his pain.'

Catherine went to a convent school near Nicholas so it meant the brother and sister still saw a lot of each other. She even built up his reputation at his boarding school by arriving with lots of pretty schoolgirls on several occasions, greatly impressing the other boys. It was particularly effective with regards to the ones that had been bullying him.

Nicholas sometimes visited Fred at his prep school down the road. 'I remember one exciting evening when Nicholas and his rebel friend, Paul, arrived in a car to see me. Wearing Ray-Bans and long duster coats, they looked like the ultimate dudes,' says Fred. 'I wanted to show the whole school that they were there for me.'

Nicholas got an A in theology in his A-levels. He had always loved the subject. Then, eager for experience in the world, he went off for a year of travelling to the US and India.

'I remember when he came back, he was very different,' says

Fred. 'I was in awe of him. He'd experienced so much and seen so many things. He'd seen real poverty and lived among it. He went away an innocent public school boy and came back as someone aware of the kind of suffering that goes on in the third world. It was to deeply affect him. He'd also given up playing the French horn and taken up the guitar, as well as smoking dope and taking acid. He'd also taken on board a Hindu approach to life, in that he wanted to live for the moment and he was aware that the ultimate search was for peace within.'

According to Catherine, when Nicholas was in Kerala tripping on acid, he thought he was Jesus and that their father was God. 'He later told me that it was hell being stuck on this trip because, once under the influence of LSD, there was no way out,' she says. Back in London, his mother was shocked by the transformation of her eldest son. He had a beard now, an Indian tan and a world-weariness that meant he was a man rather than a boy. He would never be her little boy again.

At this point, Nicholas went off to Liverpool University to read Religion. Brought up a Catholic, he could already quote the Bible verbatim, which he would use in arguments to great effect. But Nicholas' mental fragility started to show. He'd say strange things when in conversation, have a weird look in his eye and afterwards become distant and disconnected from reality. There was one incident after which Fred felt suddenly emotionally affected by his brother leaving for university again.

'I began questioning how he was and look hard for the next clue to follow,' he says. 'But there was something wrong, a weakness. There was a car waiting outside for Nicholas to take him to Liverpool and a sort of panic in the air. There was an uncertainty in Nicholas, a vulnerability.' Fred found himself in tears and not knowing why. Somehow, he had picked up on Nicholas' psychological confusion and become upset at the as yet subtle change in his brother. This was a poignant augur for the future.

Taking acid and smoking dope at university were only to increase Nicholas' mental turmoil. 'He was plagued by morbid thoughts,' says Fred. 'He was affected by Catholic guilt and sought out the Bible for forgiveness.' Good looking with his blond hair and blue eyes, he attracted plenty of girls and fell in love with one called Isabelle.

'But she left him when he was having difficulties and it broke his heart', says Fred. It was very painful for him and many of the songs that he wrote afterwards were about her. He was also starting to be obsessed by thoughts about religion.'

Catherine spent some time with him in Liverpool and one incident really disturbed her. They'd been smoking joints and went out to a nightclub. He wouldn't mix with anyone and looked as though he was on another planet. 'On the way home, he suddenly tore himself away from me and threw himself on to the pavement,' she says. 'He lay there yelling, "Can't you see I'm in pain?"' It was a distressing and telling experience. Catherine admits she was appalled and didn't know what to do. The truth was she had no idea how to handle it.

She was so worried by his behaviour and his mental state that, when she got home, she told her mother. Her mother was shocked and extremely upset, and spoke to their doctor. Nicholas was asked to come home and had to see a lot of different psychiatrists. Finally, he was diagnosed as schizophrenic, put on medication and, sadly, he had to leave university. He lived in a world of perpetual mental anguish.

'There was always a God ready to punish him,' says Catherine. 'He wanted to live as a saint. He was also prone to delusions – seeing builders digging a hole, he might conclude they were members of the IRA planting a bomb. Later, his inner demons also told him that it was a sin to have sex before marriage so he became celibate. He was tormented by these kinds of thoughts.'

Nicholas ended up on the psychiatric ward of Queen Mary's Hospital, Roehampton. 'He was put on drugs that take away your active imagination,' says Fred, who gradually came to believe that medication was not the right solution for Nicholas' problems. 'So he was aware of his basic needs like hunger and thirst, but he was lethargic and not really Nicholas. The trouble was when he got out of hospital and then decided to take himself off medication; he got all his energy back in a surge and would stay awake for three days and nights, which wasn't good either. I bumped into him once in Sheen, when he'd taken himself off medication. He was barefoot, very thin and had a mad, crazy look in his eye. It was awful.'

The argument about whether Nicholas should take drugs or not was one that caused a lot of troublesome and painful conflict in the Scott household. His parents were convinced that he should take the medication and believed that was the best strategy for his mental stability. Fred thought it removed the life force from Nicholas and that other approaches like eating well and meditating could be just as effective as drugs, without the side effects. They never came to an agreement. However, Fred did encourage Nicholas – who was himself never keen on taking his medication – to gradually cut it down, and Fred thought this was very effective.

It became obvious that Nicholas became much more stable when he got into a routine. He started taking a passionate interest in eating healthily. He even decided to fast a couple of days a week. 'He was reading some really good spiritual books at this time,' says Fred, 'and he started going to the Mormon Church, which might sound a bit weird as he's a Catholic but they were very good to him. They offered him friendship and a sense of emotional belonging when he really needed it. He also started using rosary beads as a form of meditation three times a day, which helped. He became much more at peace with himself.'

But this peace was to come and go. It was difficult for Nicholas to keep friends, but at least he had his loving family supporting him. Over the course of two years, he ended up in hospital three times, once sectioned against his will. He never wanted to be there – it was an alien world where he received drugs but no emotional support. Incredibly, psychiatric care is not always accompanied by psychotherapeutic support, the kind which would have helped him to look at his past and understand what effect it had on his present. Nevertheless, the Scott family were great at making the depressing surroundings of an NHS mental ward into a positive family experience.

'There was my father sitting on an armchair, listening to his Walkman, my mother sewing Nicholas' trousers and my brothers, Fred and Peter, took it in turn to play table tennis with him. We might as well have been at home,' says Catherine. 'I loved my family for that. They strived to make the best out of a difficult situation.'

Nicholas also derived huge pleasure from the family dog, Humphrey, a golden retriever. Nicholas would take him to the park and get a lot of comfort from his companionship and love. He also volunteered at a conservation project in Richmond Park as well as in an Oxfam shop, and eventually got his own flat in Wandsworth, through the council.

The Priory was another of his destinations for a few weeks. But he actually ran away from there. He was picked up trying to hitch-hike on a nearby dual carriageway in the middle of the night and taken back.

On one occasion, when Nicholas had stopped taking his medication, he ate some magic mushrooms with his brothers. They apparently had a mellow, creative time together. The trouble was Nicholas had to go back to his first-floor flat above one beloning to a couple who argued incessantly. Nicholas was hypersensitive and spent the whole night awake. The next day, in a manic state, he found some raw meat on the ground outside his flat and took it to the family home to cook. His mother was horrified at his psychological state and called the authorities to have him sectioned.

He was put back into Queen Mary's hospital but managed to escape to Scotland. No doubt he had fond memories of this part of Britain as the family once lived there for a few years in his youth. He called home and let them know where he was. Fred, feeling responsible because of his role in the magic-mushroom gathering and eating, took off to find his older brother. With his video camera. By this time, Fred was becoming a filmmaker.

'I had to go to a homeless hostel in Glasgow first of all,' says Fred. 'It was really grim there and Nicholas greeted me, as usual, like a beloved brother. I didn't want to just take him back home, so I thought we'd have a little adventure together. We went off to Loch Lomond and stayed in a B and B. I'd taken his guitar up for him so we could hang out and play music, then I started to film him. He was very funny on camera and would do bizarre things in an eccentric way. He was completely unaware of the camera so he came over completely naturally.' Much later, Fred ended up making this film into a documentary, which was a success with friends and other directors. It was also shown in a couple of film festivals. It showed just how close he was to his older brother. Nicholas did eventually come back home on the coach after raising some money through busking. Playing the guitar became one of his ways of surviving.

Nicholas also went on a journey to Utah, to visit a Mormon Church and congregation, but ended up homeless and destitute in New York. He had apparently decided to determine his actions by tossing a coin. He asked the coin whether to go home or to continue begging on the streets of New York. The coin told him to stay and he ended up in the Bronx in a cardboard box for a few nights. He also discovered the Bowery Mission and he was nearly thrown out for chanting from the Bible and breaking the curfew.

'Nicholas would vanish with his passport,' says Catherine, 'and get off to a good start without anyone's suspicions being aroused. About twelve hours would go by, then we would realise that Nicholas was obviously off on one of his missions again. Slowly over the next week, a search would gather momentum.' On this occasion, an uncle in Canada was brought in to find him, give him some money and get him on a flight back to the UK.

Nicholas would vanish about twice a year. The rest of the

time he occupied himself with the dog, the church, Oxfam, the conservation project and helping his sister with her children and his mother around the house. But he was also prone to dramatic mood swings. 'I often felt sorry for him,' says Catherine, 'because the dark clouds of despondency seemed to come out of nowhere. One minute, he would be happy and laughing, then he would, for no apparent reason, fall into a pit of despair. It would often be triggered by one of his thoughts, but it could be someone swearing too. He hated swearing.' Catherine once took him the book *Perfume* by Patrick Suskind, only to be greeted with fury. He thought she'd given him the book because he smelled bad.

In one of his episodes away, Nicholas had set out on a trip to Lourdes, which turned out to be one of his more dangerous adventures. 'He was determined to go to the Grotto in Lourdes and decided to go via Nice in the south of France,' says Catherine. Nicholas, oblivious to the potential risks, stopped to dive into the sea, leaving his wallet with his money, his passport and all his clothes, including his shoes, on the beach. When he got out of the sea, everything had been stolen, leaving Nicholas with only a pair of shabby boxer shorts to his name. Fortunately, he met a tramp, who helped him out by giving him a pair of jeans and a T-shirt. He had to resort to begging because his guitar had been stolen so he couldn't even busk. Soon he was starving and penniless. He stowed away on a boat going to Sardinia but he was caught and sent back to France. He recounted that the captain and crew were kind to him and offered him their food and drink. Not that any of these experiences persuaded Nicholas to give up on his trip.

'Lourdes was always a place Nicholas was inextricably drawn to. His devotion to the Virgin Mary was greater than to God, I think,' says Catherine. 'Nicholas is possibly the only person I know, however, who would have the sheer courage to actually sleep in the Grotto.' After two nights there, a security guard discovered him. Nicholas was starving and phoned home to ask for help. His mother went into instant action, getting in touch with a Catholic priest who recommended a hostel where he could stay for a couple of nights. Money was sent to him at the local post office and he got a flight home. He arrived back two stone lighter and shattered.

Nicholas tried to commit suicide twice. Once he overdosed on his medication. Luckily, there were only 12 pills left and he was taken to hospital to have his stomach pumped almost immediately. This seemed to be more of a protest than a true suicide attempt.

He did the same thing two weeks later. Catherine says, 'He told me that he had a vision of lying in Richmond Park, in a little glade, gazing up into the blue sky and very slowly falling into a deep sleep that would last for ever.' So he went and bought some paracetamol and a large bottle of Vimto. He took 60 of these tablets and then he lay in the cool grass and waited for that long-lasting, delicious sleep, death.

'The strange thing is,' she says, 'he later explained that he felt far from tired. In fact, he felt more energised than he had ever felt in his life and suddenly he realised that the last thing he wanted to do was to die. He started to run through the park in a terrible panic and was relieved to quickly find two policewomen on their rounds who, seeing the anxiety on his face, asked if he was OK. They called an ambulance and

Nicholas was whisked off to Roehampton Hospital where, after a long wait, he had his stomach pumped yet again.'

The flat and independent living were becoming too much for him because of the couple downstairs who fought a lot. It disturbed him. He was a sensitive man. He even reported them to the police, but then he became convinced the couple knew. He lived in terror that he would somehow be punished by them. In the end, Nicholas moved back home to the warmth and safety of his parents' house.

Nicholas was living a solitary existence. 'His room at home was like a monk's cell,' says Catherine. 'And he had very few possessions, plus he never spent a penny on himself. His clothes were all from Oxfam and he owned, I think, only one pair of shoes, a pair of old brogues. He had many rosaries, Bibles and books about Mormons, one photo album, some old letters and, of course, his beloved guitar. His flat was full of hand-me-downs from the whole family. That was literally the sum total of his belongings. Material ownership simply held no value for him. Despite that, he fantasised about winning the lottery. It was a strange dichotomy: there was no doubt that he would have loved to have had the money but, without it, he saw no need to possess anything at all.'

Nicholas was having a better year in 2003. 'He was leading a good life,' says Fred. 'He was off the medication and that gave him renewed energy. He was working at Oxfam. He was still exploring religion but he had decided the Mormons were not for him and he returned more to his old faith, Catholicism.

'He had strict daily routines, which he adhered to on a strict basis, and wrote lists endlessly,' says Catherine. A typical list read:

Missing

What to do today, Lord?
Bathe
Scriptures
Feed birds
Purchase rye bread
Work for an hour or two
Library to obtain card
Lewis and picture of Lord
Prayer and meditation
Go and see Javed

He also wrote lists of all the things he appreciated:

Thank you list
Hope, great hope
Roux's rosary beads
Books and knowledge
Thinking crystals
Friends, relations and children
Occupation and labour
Richmond Park and Richmond

Everyone in the family thought Nicholas seemed to be leading a relatively normal life. Everything seemed good. There was no indication that he was about to disappear. But that he did, on 17 March 2003, eventually emailing Fred to let the family know that he was on his way to Medjugorje in Bosnia. He chose this destination because there is a famous shrine to the Virgin Mary there. Apparently, six people have seen visions of her since 1981 and millions of pilgrims have visited the spot.

Nicholas wrote in his diary, 'I set out for Medjugorje on Saint Patrick's Day 2003, thinking perhaps that I may never return to England because of the volatile times I had envisaged there. Indeed, as I reposed after Mass in Westminster Abbey, I thought I saw a murderer staring at me and realised I had to leave.' Images that tumbled destructively around Nicholas' head were not the ones that appeared in the outside world.

Fred was in New York when Nicholas disappeared this time and he got an email from Nicholas, saying, 'Remember to say "Gentle Jesus".' Fred's quickfire, affirmative response was, 'Jesus is my homeboy.' He soon found out where Nicholas was. Again, Fred set off to find his brother. Again, he took his camera and made a film. He found Nicholas by chance, sitting in the local post office, but 'he had crazed eyes and I had to remind him that I was his brother. Medjugorje is quite a strange place. I found it to be full of fear. It was like a Disneyland for religious people.' Nicholas was struggling with hardly any money. He was staying in a marquee on his own, but claimed, 'I'm used to being poor. It's good training for the soul. It's like a necessary penance.'

Nicholas was begging for money and was content that the Virgin Mary was such a strong presence in the Bosnian town. While he was there, he remembered all the songs he'd ever learned on his guitar and all the poetry he knew, and he was walking a lot. He was thin but enjoying himself. As usual when Fred arrived, the brothers went on a mini-adventure. They had money for beds in hostels and went on a trip to Mostar, which had been the scene of horrific bloodbaths during the Bosnian war. While they had Nicholas' brogues repaired there, he insisted on walking around with bare feet.

Eventually, Fred asked him to consider his options – which were either to stay there permanently without any money but with spiritual fulfilment, or to come back to his warm, loving family. It was time to make that vital decision. Nicholas opted for home, as usual.

In June 2003, Nicholas went on a family holiday to Devon with Catherine, her children and her husband, Tim. She remarks that Nicholas seemed preoccupied, although he did do one telling thing by giving her a precious photo album and a diary, asking her to keep it 'after he'd gone'. Catherine didn't suspect anything because he was always going and coming back.

On this trip, Nicholas was so distracted that he forgot to keep an eye on his nephew, four-year-old Henry, which caused a panic because the little boy was left alone on the sands. Nicholas enjoyed playing Scrabble in the evening but spent the days in a 'dark suit, striding down the beach with his Bible aloft, proclaiming quietly to himself'. Catherine felt quite distanced and irritated by him, and was glad to say goodbye. It was an attitude she was to dramatically change, as it turned out that her view of Nicholas going off to get a train back to London would be the last glimpse of him that she would ever have. 'Now I look back on those final moments with him and wish I could have them back again and behave very differently,' she says. 'I have not seen him since. I miss him.'

In retrospect, Fred says he realises that Nicholas had been secretly planning a big trip on his own for a long time. 'He was saving up money,' he says, 'and took out a bank loan for £4,000. He'd had enough of Wandsworth – he wanted to travel. After all, his trip to India was one of his best life experiences.'

His diary entry for 15 July reads:

Get dressed
Observe atlas and road map
Listen and pray in darkness – Mozart, Faure,
Chingchong hymns
Read a wee bit
Cleanse garments for an hour in silent prayer
6.30am – crash until 8.30am
Bathe
Depart

His mother recalls that final morning because he kept coming in and out of the living room while she was teaching a French student English. The student said 'goodbye' and that gave Nicholas the opportunity to say it too. She heard the door click and Nicholas was gone. And he didn't come back.

During the first week, nobody in the family was particularly worried. A few days later, they found a note in his room, saying, 'I am going away for some time. I don't know when I will be coming back.'

It usually took Nicholas three weeks to make contact when he went missing. But this time the three weeks passed and there was no telephone call. His family also found out about that £4,000 bank loan and discovered two withdrawals – one was in Paris for £70 and the other was on 21 July, in Ancona, Italy, for £150. Ancona was where he'd taken the boat for Bosnia in March, so they suspected that he had returned to Medjugorje. Fred went off to find him again, but this time he didn't succeed. Nicholas was nowhere to be seen.

Inexplicably, there were no more withdrawals from his bank account and now the family were in crisis over his disappearance. His parents contacted the charity Missing People, various embassies, Interpol, the police and the British Red Cross, all without success. Fred tried emailing him but there was no response. This time, Nicholas had really disappeared. Everyone was distraught. They'd got so used to him going away for relatively brief times that they never imagined he would literally disappear.

An Italian TV programme on missing people, *Chi L'ha visto?* (*Have you Seen Them?*), included a story on Nicholas. The researchers said that the key to success in that kind of case was to find a cluster of sightings to suggest the missing person was staying in the same place for a certain length of time. But sightings of Nicholas were disparate and so sadly not taken seriously by the production team. They felt they didn't have enough evidence to act on.

Determined to do something, Nicholas' father went out to Italy on 27 October and, accompanied by government officials, checked hospitals and refuges around Ancona. There were false sightings, like a member of the police who said he'd seen someone who looked like Nicholas praying on a mat beside the road. The TV crew from *Chi L'ha Visto?* made another programme with Nicholas' father. There were supposed sightings of Nicholas walking up mountains wearing crucifixes or along beaches but, frustratingly, none of them turned out to be him. It was terribly disappointing for the family – hope would arrive then vanish just as quickly.

However, the family at this stage remained convinced that Nicholas was just ahead of them and that they would definitely find him. The general feeling among them was that at least Nicholas was in a warm coastal climate and among the kind people of southern Italy, and that this TV programme would find them in the end. Hope was in their hearts where they were forcing it to stay.

Fred was flown over to Italy by the TV production team and he found two Franciscan monks who said they'd seen Nicholas in Assisi. 'I thought it was true because Nicholas is really interested in St Francis of Assisi,' he says. 'In fact, he could quite easily be modelling himself on him. St Francis didn't have any money and lived on gifts from others. This information struck a chord with me.'

Fred even gave a live broadcast on Italian TV on Nicholas' birthday, which was 5 December. He found himself in the middle of huge screens projecting images of his brother's face. It was a powerful experience and Fred was absolutely desperate to find his brother at this point. 'You don't understand the enormity of it' he said to his sister. 'If I were to find him, it would be incredible.'

Fred's video footage of Nicholas playing cricket, proclaiming from the Bible on the rooftops of East Sheen and getting his shoes repaired in Mostar made a powerful story. Fred even felt moved to say that, at times, he felt that 'Nicholas was doing something quite special by going missing and telling no one where he was; that he had found a way of putting his religious message across to millions of people in Italy.' But there were still not enough sightings to convince the production team that Nicholas was in Italy and, sadly but inevitably, they didn't make any more programmes on him.

The family spent Christmas 2003 together and, of course,

remembered missing Nicholas. Their father made a speech saying they were all praying for him. By New Year, there'd been a significant shift in the family perspective. Somehow, they seemed to accept that Nicholas was really missing. Independently, they would all at times wonder whether Nicholas was dead, then something would happen that would fill them with hope again. They accepted that he was missing but not that he'd gone for good.

During 2004, Catherine consulted with various mediums who told her a variety of different stories. One thought Nicholas was in Glasgow and still alive, while a douser called Daphne wanted a sample of Nicholas' handwriting as well as something he would have handled many times, a map indicating the precise location where he had been seen and a map showing where his last financial transaction had taken place. 'She dangled a piece of my brother's clothing on the map and it apparently showed her the route he had taken. She said she thought he was still alive and that he had headed for Barcelona and was living in a small village in northern Spain,' says Catherine.

This was to prompt a search by Fred on a bike in the area that summer. 'I decided to do a pilgrimage along the Camino de Santiago in northern Spain,' he says. 'It took six weeks. Then I went down to Fatima in Portugal, because Nicholas wrote a lot in emails about this religious place. I didn't find Nicholas but I did change my perceptions about God and Catholicism. I actually had magical experiences looking for Nicholas and I think that's his gift to me. Fatima was a very spiritual place and I actually felt touched by the Holy Spirit there. I would never have been open for an experience like that before this journey.'

A third medium thought Nicholas was dead. She saw a boat and had a strong sense of criminal intent around him. In the end, they all had different messages and none of them came up with anything concrete.

On 5 December 2005, the family decided to have a 'Thinking of Nicholas' service in the Falklands Memorial Chapel in London, to mark his 33rd birthday. They sang his favourite hymns, read from his favourite texts and listened to some choral music he would have loved. They were letting him know that they were all still thinking about him; it was also a kind of elegy to him whether he was alive or dead. Their father's prayer for his son ended, 'But let us here today, on your birthday, contemplate anew the prospect that you are still alive here on earth and pray that you are in a state of fulfilled contentment among people that care for you. And that you may live out your life more free than before, free from doubts and despairs, in a steady state of personal grace and joy.'

In October 2006, Fred visited a Franciscan refuge in Italy and found a guestbook with Nicholas' name in it for the period January–March 2004. Fred believes that Nicholas is fine, living out his life the way he wants to do it. 'He's living like a saint,' he says. 'I don't doubt that those sorts of miracles can happen.' The rest of the family are holding onto this information with their hands on their hearts.

(Names have been changed in this story)

Chapter Eleven

My Dream Came True When I Found My Half-brothers

Anna Cameron, curvy, brown-haired and 24, has had a life that has been hard to bear. She's had to fight the demons of her rocky childhood to survive. It hasn't been easy, but Anna is a survivor. She also had 3 children by the time she was 19.

Anna grew up in the north-west of England with hardly any memories of her father, Roger. Her mother, Karen, 47, managed finally to escape this extraordinarily violent man by the time Anna was three. 'I didn't know anything about his insanely vicious behaviour,' Anna says, sadly. 'I hardly remember anything about him. I remember him being fat and his response once when I wanted some clip-on earrings and I was very, very young. Mum said, "No," and dad said something like, "You tight bitch, get her some earrings." I didn't realise until recently that he was actually taking all mum's benefit money so she didn't have any money. He was a horrible man but I didn't realise that until recently either.'

For many of Anna's 24 years, she missed her father terribly. She didn't understand who he was or what he was like, but she missed him as someone she thought would be an emotionally loving parent. In the last two years, she has discovered the truth behind these little-girl longings, which accompanied her into adulthood. The truth has been unpalatable and painful, especially for a daughter who wanted her father to be a healthy, affectionate, warm human being. It was not to be.

Anna grew up without photos or a mention of her father. She always asked questions but hardly ever got any answers. 'My mum got together with him just after he'd split up with his first wife and he already had two sons. One of those sons, Christopher, did become part of our lives because he visited our house a lot,' she says, 'and I have now seen dad's first wedding photo when he was thin. I really wanted to look at photos of him because people always said I didn't look like my mum, so I assumed I looked like my dad. I spent a lot of my childhood asking questions about my dad. I couldn't stand not being with him, but I didn't understand what he was really like. It's taken me a long time to get all the right information. I have a younger sister, Gemma, but she doesn't seem to be so badly affected.'

There is another memory of him from her childhood that is more pertinent. 'I was in Mum's arms and we had to run away from him,' she says. 'We ended up hiding in some long grass in a field so that he couldn't find us.' Although Anna doesn't seem to remember how frightening this occasion was, it must have affected her emotionally. Even a toddler knows when their mother is terrified by her father.

Bullied, attacked and cowed into submission by this violent

man, Anna's mother, Karen, tried to escape several times. But he was determined to keep her in line. 'Mum tried to stand up for herself from time to time. Once, when I was tiny, Mum decided to answer my dad back and he threatened to kill her,' she explains. 'I don't remember any of this, but she called the police, they came and my dad managed to persuade them that it was her who was unstable and on tablets. He was a nasty piece of work but I didn't know that for a very long time.'

On another occasion, her mother got away to her own mother's place in Lancashire. She took her children – it was the only solution she could think of. 'My dad, who was manipulative and possessive, found my mother's brother and bribed him with money to tell him where we were. He found us again and forced her to come back. It was terrible for her.'

Finally, her mother got away, when Anna was three. 'She upped and went with Gemma and I,' says Anna. 'We went to a women's refuge. There's a photograph of me with a school folder and I'm starting nursery. We had loads of kids to play with. It wasn't a bad experience. Mum was relieved but she was also heartbroken. She loved him and you can't just shut off love. She loved him and hated him all at the same time. Mind you, I only know this from what she tells me now. At the time, she put on a brave face for us children. Dad wasn't mentioned again until I was about eight. That's when I started asking all the questions.'

Anna has spent much of her life dreaming about finding her real dad and her half-brothers. 'I used to yearn to find them all,' she says. 'I wanted to have a dad and I would have loved to have had my older half-brothers around. Christopher used to babysit for us and, apparently, when I was two, I used to shout, "Don't go, my Christopher," at him when he was leaving. I already loved him when he was eleven and coming to babysit for us. I knew I had another half-brother but I didn't know him. It was all about safety. I wanted to feel safe in the world.'

Eight months after going to the women's refuge, they were allocated a council house. 'Mum met another man, who was called Mike, through the neighbours,' says Anna. 'He was a nice man but he wasn't very well; he had diabetes and a bad liver. I went on to call him "Dad" and we did treat him like that. We got to know all his family very well. The only trouble was, he didn't have much time for us because he was ill a lot of the time.'

Mike owned a barge and this made a significant difference to Anna's quality of life for a few years. 'That barge was a godsend,' she says. 'We would all go on holidays on the canals. I'd never been on holiday before. We'd have six weeks' holiday in summer and we'd go on the barge for the whole time. It was magical. Mike would take us to Wales. We'd take friends with us. I have some of my best childhood memories of being on that barge.'

At one point, they moved out nearer to Anna's grandmother. 'I think Mum wanted to get away,' she says. 'She had too many bad memories from where we used to live. Mike did help me with my homework quite a lot and I remember he taught me how to spell "ambidextrous" when I was eight. I've done that with my own children. His brother, Clive, used to come round too and he'd read stories to us. That was good too. I remember Uncle Clive teaching me to swing by myself when we were on a barge trip and we'd stopped at a park. That felt important at the time.'

Anna called Mike her dad but she was still wondering about her real father – questions kept coming to her: What he was like? Was she like him? Where was he now? But nobody was giving her any answers. Her mother and Mike split up not long after they had a son, Eddie, who is now 17.

'Mum just said she didn't want to be with Mike any longer,' says Anna. 'I think she was probably having to look after him quite a lot because he had a bad liver and diabetes and wasn't very well. I didn't want him to go. He wasn't my real dad but he was the man we called "Dad" and the idea of him not being around made me unhappy.'

She was only nine and she'd already had two father figures disappear out of her life. 'I remember him saying he didn't want to go but he had to accept it because my mum didn't want him around any longer,' she says. 'And as he left and I was crying, he said he would have taken me and my sister with him if we'd been his children. Again, I didn't really understand – one minute he was there and the next minute he'd gone.'

Eddie did actually go and live with him. 'Poor Eddie had to grow up before his time,' says Anna, 'because he looked after Mike more and more, who gradually deteriorated and died six years ago, weighing only four stone. It was very sad.'

Anna started dwelling on her own father again. She started plying her mother with questions. Now her mother told her something that would haunt her for years. 'I asked where my real dad was,' she says, 'and Mum told me that he had died. I was shocked that she hadn't told me before. Now I knew I would never meet him or be with him.' Anna's fantasy was blown apart. Now she realised that her real dad was never going to live up to her imagined ideal of him. He was dead.

She had to accept that particular dream was over. When she found out much later what really happened to her dad, she was plunged headlong into another sort of absolute horror and grief. Especially because she thought her mother hadn't told her the truth.

Primary schools came and went for Anna, like many of the other unstable parts of her life. 'I was always starting new schools,' she says, 'which was nerve-wracking. It made me very shy. People would always comment on my big blue eyes and I'd hide. I was embarrassed. I was best at art and writing stories at school but I had a big problem asking for help. That was my downfall. I didn't find out properly what I was supposed to be doing, then I was too afraid to ask for help.'

When Anna was ten, she found her first sweetheart at school. 'We held hands a lot,' she says. 'His name was Peter and he took care of me. He was a gentleman.' By the time she was 11, she'd met Richard, who ended up becoming the father of all her children. 'We used to hang out together; we were like best mates. In fact, there was a time when he was seeing both me and my sister, Gemma,' she says. 'But he went out with me and would become the love of my life.'

Her mother found a new boyfriend, who was to play a huge role in another downward spiral for Anna. 'This man would get a packet of dolly mixtures and persuade me or my sister to sit on his knee,' says Anna. 'Then he would touch us underneath our skirts. It was disgusting and very frightening. I was too nervous to tell Mum because I didn't want to destroy her relationship with him but we were children and that shouldn't have been happening. There were even nights when I heard him open the door of our bedroom and look in. I think if there hadn't been two of us there, one of us would have suffered even worse serious sexual abuse. Gemma and I talked about it and, eventually, we did tell our mum. She was horrified and called the police.'

As the relationship collapsed, the case went to court but he wasn't convicted because there was too little evidence. 'I was scared and let Gemma do all the talking,' she says. 'I felt really bad about that afterwards. I believed for a long time that he'd got off because I hadn't testified against him. But he got off because there wasn't enough evidence to convict him.' Anna also felt guilty for leaving Gemma with the burden of giving evidence against him.

By the time Anna got to secondary school, she was heading for difficult times. Although she was in the top-stream classes, she didn't like it there because her friends were in the lower classes. She didn't care about academic achievement but she did care about being around her friends. 'I started bunking off from school because I didn't like the students in my classes,' she says. 'I wasn't going into school, which meant I was hanging round the streets and getting into other sorts of trouble.'

Her mother had also found another boyfriend, called Tom, who was bad news. 'I was about twelve. I walked in and there she was sitting on his knee,' she says. 'I asked what they were doing and she explained that they were together and that was it. He was a bully. He used to take all her benefits.' Again, for Anna it meant more instability at home and having to get used to another man.

Not surprisingly, she reacted badly. 'He was horrible to my mum,' she says, 'so I hated it. I also went off the rails at school. I was hardly going in. I was arrested for stealing £200 of make-up. I started slashing my arms because I was in such emotional pain. I also expected Tom to abuse me – I didn't trust men. I was drinking. It was a terrible time.'

Tom managed to start an affair with a woman across the road. After seeing her, he'd come back and search out Anna's mum again. Eventually, she fell pregnant. At first, he said he wanted to have the baby, but he disappeared never to be seen again. Which was probably a fortunate turn of events. At that point, Karen decided to start going to church – it provided stability in the quagmire of bad relationships that she'd been in.

'She found another man, called Nigel, who was a friend's brother,' says Anna. 'He was actually a nice man. He said he would take on her children, including the new baby, Charlie, and he also had a good job making parts for heavy machinery. Mum is still with Nigel, ten years later. I didn't like him. I just wanted my real dad. I felt I couldn't trust any of these men that were with my mum. I'd had too many bad experiences, so I gave Nigel a really hard time. I was very badly behaved. I didn't want him around.'

It wasn't long after Nigel appeared on the scene that Anna got pregnant at 14. 'Richard and I plus some of our friends had gone round to one of their houses,' she explained, 'and we were messing around sexually. I wasn't a virgin but I hadn't had very much experience of sex. We didn't really have sex, which is why I didn't think I could be pregnant. I didn't think that Richard had ejaculated inside me.'

Anna did a pregnancy test about a week later and it came up negative, so she was reassured. 'I didn't realise you can't do a pregnancy test until it's your period time,' she says. 'Mum never talked about contraception – it was too embarrassing. I thought

I was OK but then I started being sick at school. My friend said I was pregnant and I refused to believe her. But we went to a young person's information centre to find out in our lunch break. I did the pregnancy test again and it was confirmed that I was pregnant.'

She was scared and shocked. Anna couldn't face the idea of telling her mum. So she persuaded her friend to phone her mother and tell her instead. 'Mum told me to come home and I went,' she says. 'I was crying and saying I would get rid of the baby, but Mum was certain that it wasn't right to have an abortion. So I went ahead with the pregnancy.'

Richard didn't believe that he was responsible so they fell out. Richard's mother was equally adamant that it wasn't Richard's baby. 'He was sixteen, I was fourteen. We didn't know how to talk through our problems and differences so we stopped speaking to one another,' she says. 'Then soon afterwards, I met another boy, Steve, who was eighteen and said he would take on the baby.'

Anna was still at school. In fact, she says getting pregnant had a calming effect on her unruly behaviour. 'I calmed down and started studying,' she says. 'I stopped smoking and drinking. I started taking care of my body; I wasn't going to let anything affect my baby. In fact, being pregnant made me very popular at school. Everyone wanted to talk to me about it. I got milk tokens and I was always drinking milk.'

Her mother was with her when she gave birth to Ellie at 15. 'I was still with Steve,' she says, 'but I wanted my mum at the hospital. I also shed a few tears because I wanted Richard to be there too. After all, he was the father. Ellie was a big baby; she was eight pounds, eight ounces, and I was badly torn as a result. Steve didn't even realise I'd given birth – he was at work.'

She had left school by this time. 'They'd offered to have me back,' she says, 'but I didn't want anyone else to look after my baby. Mind you, it was very hard. Ellie wouldn't sleep and she started losing weight. I started to get depressed because I wasn't coping well with her. I came close to having her adopted. I was pretty desperate.' Anna's mum helped her out a lot at this stage.

'It got better when Ellie was about one,' says Anna. 'But then Steve and I split up. He got into trouble. He was caught stealing from a petrol station so he was sent home to live with his mother. He felt like he couldn't carry on because he was living apart from me. I thought we could have managed. In the end, he sent back all the pictures of Ellie and I, and then I was hurt. I thought he could have kept at least a photo of Ellie. After all, he had promised to take her on as his own. I found out afterwards that he was already seeing someone else at this stage.'

Soon afterwards, Richard and Anna started talking to each other again. They had Ellie and there was a part of both of them that wanted to make their relationship work. 'Richard and I decided to make a go of it,' she says, 'and we were given our first council house when I was nearly sixteen. It was round the corner from my mum and she had to be the guarantor for it. We were very happy to get our own place at such a young age.'

Anna also started going to a centre for teenagers and women who were having difficulty coping with their babies.

'They did help me out. We talked about what problems we were having with our babies and they encouraged me to do more with Ellie. But at this stage, I got pregnant with Christina and they told me that the best idea was to have an abortion. They said it would be best for me and I disagreed. I didn't want to get rid of my baby. I was with Richard, whom I loved, and it was my choice what I did.'

At 17, Anna gave birth to Christina. 'My waters broke at a friend's house and Richard didn't believe me, but we got to hospital,' she says. 'Richard kept making excuses to leave the room because he was so nervous. At one point, we were both crying. It was very emotional. And Christina didn't take long to arrive. Richard rang round and all the family turned up. It was a very special day. I'll always remember it.'

But they had to ask the council if they could move because they were having problems with a boy that Richard knew. 'This boy wanted money for drugs and he kept turning up at the door,' she says. 'He was so angry that he would kick in the front door and I knew Ellie might have been nearby. I couldn't live like that. We swapped houses with a woman who had a gorgeous place, which was perfect.'

Anna and Richard weren't thinking about contraception during this time. 'I lost a baby,' she says, unable to stop the tears, 'and that was really painful. I could feel that something wasn't right. The people at the hospital told me to keep whatever came in a tube that they gave me, so I did. Then I had to take it into them. It was my baby and they started prodding it right there and then in front of me. I hated that. It upset me. I was depressed after that.'

At 18, she was pregnant again with a son, Aaron. 'I was nervous all through this pregnancy that I was going to lose my baby,' she says. But he was OK. Richard was a proud father and he'd also found a job at a company that made equipment for schools, where he went on to become a manager.

They struggled with money, but the kids never suffered. 'I wasn't really having a very good relationship with my mum at this time,' she says. 'I still didn't like Nigel. He wasn't my birth father. I didn't trust him after all the other men in my mum's life and so I blamed my mum. When Richard started work, it was difficult coping with three children but there was a part of me that liked it. We were a little gang. We could do our own thing. We didn't have to answer to anyone. We'd watch TV and eat sweets if we wanted to.'

However, Richard started being more difficult to pin down. He was working during the day, then going out at night. 'He didn't want to be at home with us,' she says. 'I didn't know what to do. He was being selfish but he was only young. He was twenty-one and was probably finding it hard having a girlfriend and three children.'

Anna got pregnant with her fourth child and decided that she had enough. 'I was nineteen, I had three children and I knew having a fourth one would be too much,' she says. 'I made my mind up that I would have an abortion. But I blamed Richard for getting me pregnant. I blamed him for not being more careful when we had sex. Unfortunately, we didn't talk about all of this and, somehow, this all led to more misunderstanding between us. We weren't being affectionate towards one another and our relationship broke down.'

Sadly, Anna and Richard parted company. 'Aaron was one and a half,' she says. 'We'd had four years together. We were childhood sweethearts and it was over. We did try to get back together again several times but we couldn't get it to work.'

Anna and Richard did manage to sit down and have an adult conversation about the children.

'We arranged that Richard could come and see the kids when he wanted,' she says, 'and that he would have them at weekends. It was a very good arrangement and we stuck to it. There were times when watching him walking down the path was the hardest thing I would ever do, but it was over and there was nothing I could do about it.'

They settled down into their new routine and, if Anna had problems coping with the children, Richard would always come over. 'He was good like that,' she says. 'But I started thinking about the two half-brothers who were my dad's sons. I knew my dad was dead but I started dreaming about these older brothers, how I'd love to be in contact with them. It was almost as if they would be my saviours. The trouble was I didn't know where they were or their dates of birth.'

She started to think about taking action. 'I'd been thinking about them in the back of my mind for years,' she says, 'but when I was younger, I had no idea what to do in order to find them. I didn't know about the internet, or the Salvation Army. Then at twenty, as soon as I had access to a computer, I found companies who would trace your family, but they all cost a lot of money, so there was nothing I could do. I didn't have any extra money to spend on it.'

At 21, Anna had started to do a little job. She ran a clothes stall for the single mothers' group that she attended. 'My mum worked there as well,' she says, 'and that Christmas, we were talking and I was still thinking about my dad and my brothers. I asked her how my dad died and she told me he'd had cancer. She also started to tell me a few horrific stories about him and what he did to her, like the time he threw a coffee table at her. I started to realise how awful he was. Then I asked her about my half-brothers and told her how much I longed to meet them and have them in my life. She suggested going to the Salvation Army because they had a family-tracing service, I had no idea that this service existed.'

Finally, Anna called into the Salvation Army office and got hold of the forms to trace her half-brothers. 'But this form had lots of questions that I didn't know the answers to,' she says, 'which meant I didn't feel confident enough to send it in. I kept it for ages in the back of a cupboard. But months later, I thought, What harm can it do? I'll just send the form in with the dates of birth that I had managed to find and see what happens.'

Something did happen. Two days before Christmas 2005, out of the blue, Anna received the phone call that she'd hoped she would receive for years. 'There was no intermediary conversation with the Salvation Army,' she says. 'I just heard this bloke on the end of the phone saying, "This is Christopher. How are you?" I thought it was some kind of sick joke. I couldn't believe it could possibly be true. This was my biggest dream come true. I had found my half-brothers.'

Anna was 22 and at last she was in touch with some of the men in her family. She was ecstatic. They talked and talked about the past, their memories and their dad. That was the difficult bit. 'While we were talking, Christopher said something that really upset me,' she says. 'We were discussing our dad and his death at one point, and then Christopher told me that he'd killed himself. I was beside myself inside. I thought my mother had been keeping it a secret. Inside, I crumbled. My dad had committed suicide and nobody had thought to tell me the truth. I was so happy to find my half-brothers, but I was destroyed by that piece of information.'

Anna ran round to her best friend's house. 'She was having a bath and she was so happy for me. She knew how much finding my half-brothers meant to me,' says Anna. Next, she phoned her mother, who didn't seem that happy for her. 'Now I realise that all this activity around my half-brothers was bringing back memories of my violent father for her,' she says. 'But at the time, I thought she was being mean. I mentioned that I knew that he had committed suicide and she quickly changed the subject. This was a difficult time for my mother and me.'

Anna was angry with her mother because she thought she hadn't told her the truth about her father's suicide. Later, she discovered that her mother hadn't known either. All her fantasies about her dad had come crashing down around her, one by one. This was a man that she'd missed and yearned for in her childhood. Now she had not only discovered that he'd killed himself, but also what a horrible man he'd been. It wasn't easy. She'd found her half-brothers – which was fantastic for her – but she'd also been plunged into despair around her father.

Christopher phoned again. 'I wanted to go and meet them right away,' says Anna, 'but my brothers live in Cornwall. Christopher is thirty-four and a chef, with four children, and Simon is twenty-six, with no ties. But I hadn't realised how expensive it was to get there. When they said a train ticket would cost £106, my hopes were dashed. I couldn't afford it. Again, I would have to wait. It was frustrating.'

But she had a saviour in the unexpected form of her ex, Richard. 'One day a few weeks later, Richard handed me an envelope on which he'd written, "To Anna, I'm so glad to be able to make your dreams come true." Inside he'd put the £106 that I needed to buy a train ticket to Cornwall. That totally blew me away and touched my heart. There's still a lot of love between Richard and I, and that was so kind of him. He knew how important it was for me to meet my brothers.'

Anna took the seven-hour train ride to St Austell in March 2005. 'Richard had the children,' she says. 'And I was a nervous wreck, wondering what it would be like to be with my half-brothers. I talked non-stop to strangers on the way there. I couldn't sit still. When I got off the train, I could see two men but I pretended I hadn't. I was embarrassed. They came up to me and Christopher said, "You haven't changed since you were a baby."'

That broke the ice. 'We ended up in the pub,' she says, 'and there were some awkward silences but, after a few drinks, we couldn't stop talking. The weekend flew by. I was really interested in finding out about our dad so they told me all sorts of disturbing stories about what a brute he was. He'd kicked their mum badly when she had little Simon in her arms. Christopher also remembers staying with our family and hearing my mum shouting, "No!" in the night, then getting up in the morning and seeing her face was black and blue. It was hard to listen to. I felt torn in two, by the need to hear about my dad, but by the horror of what I was hearing.'

Their father had died in Cornwall nearby and Anna felt like she wanted to go and see his grave. 'My brothers hadn't been to this cemetery for eleven years, but I felt the urge to go,' she says. 'When we got there, we couldn't find his grave. I ended up putting the flowers I'd brought on someone else's grave.

Christopher also gave me a talking to. He said, "Anna, if you're grieving over Dad, then don't. He was a brute. Your mother did you a huge favour by getting you away from him." That hurt because it was a truth that I was having difficulty with.'

However, Anna came away from the weekend knowing she had two half-brothers who would stand by her. 'It went too fast,' she says, 'but it was great. I didn't want to leave them. Christopher shouted, "I don't want you to go." They had found a little sister and I had found two big brothers, which made me feel more secure in the world.'

Simon, the quieter one, has since moved up north to be around Anna and her kids. 'Last year, I had messages from both of them, saying "Happy Birthday". That felt so new and brilliant.' But it hasn't all been a simple transition. For a year, Anna had nightmares about her father and fell into a depression over the end of her fantasy about him.

'I couldn't bear the pain,' she says. 'I couldn't stop crying. I started cutting myself on the back of my hands and across my face. I isolated myself from everyone. I wasn't speaking to my mother. I was just about coping with the kids but it was very hard. Simon was around all this time, helping me out – he was great. He'd tell me he loved his little sister and that really helped.'

On Mother's Day 2007, Anna found herself making a card. She still wasn't speaking to her mother because she thought she'd betrayed her over her dad's death. In Anna's mind, her mother had allowed her to live with a lie for 11 years. 'I'd made this card,' she says, 'and I hadn't intended to give it to my mother. But in the end I thought, I've made it for her, I'll give it to her. She was at the centre where I was and I persuaded my friend to give it to my mum. She came over crying and saying, "Thank you so much." Since then, our relationship has gone from strength to strength. Now it's better than it's ever been.'

At 24, Anna has three children that she adores – despite the financial hardship, they are getting on fine. Richard is a manager at his company now and still a good father. She has a good relationship with her mother and she has finally come to terms with who her father was and what he did. He is no longer a fantasy figure. 'I understand how tough it was for my mum and how horrific he was to her,' she says. 'So I see what it took her to get us away from him and how good for us that was. I'd always somehow thought she'd deprived us of having a dad. Now I see she saved us from his violence.'

Anna has also accepted her mum's partner, Nigel. 'That was the final part of the jigsaw puzzle,' she says. 'He'd always wanted a daughter and I refused to be it. I'd always wanted a father but I'd always refused to let him be it. I sent him a text, saying I was really glad it had turned out this way and I'd been searching desperately for a father when he'd been there all the time. I know he was moved by that message.'

But the icing on the cake is having Christopher and Simon around. 'At last they are here and Simon is living with me at the moment,' says Anna. 'My life has been transformed by finding them. I'm content at last.'

(All names in this story have been changed)

Chapter Twelve

I Ran Away and Hated It

Beautiful, trendy 16-year-old, Sarah Ross, has enormous brown eyes and a radiant smile. But sometimes you wonder where she gets the strength to keep smiling. She has her own unique sense of style and she's had to call on that individuality to survive.

You wouldn't know it from her lovely dark, curly hair and great clothes, but she has had a life that has taken so many traumatic twists and turns, it's hard to imagine how she has been able to keep a grip on reality and avoided ending up on a psychiatric ward. To be honest, she couldn't avoid being scarred by her short, troubled life, but Sarah is a survivor and that shows both in her smile and how she's dealing with her difficulties. She's confronting them in order to release herself from them and she's getting some good support.

She was born in 1991 in Manchester, the second daughter of Sharon. Even her birth was marked by a distressing event.

'While Mum was in hospital having me,' explains Sarah, 'my dad was seeing someone else. My mum broke up with him when she discovered what was going on. That was the beginning of my life.'

When Sharon took the girls home from hospital, their father had left. But they settled down and, for a few years, the girls felt nurtured. Then Sharon met Pete, who unfortunately was using heroin, and she went on to follow his lead. 'She was only twenty-five and she went off with Pete, which led to her heroin habit. It was a disaster for me and my sister, Sally, who is four years older than me,' says Sarah. 'But at least we had my nanny there and she would do anything for us. We didn't see so much of Mum at that time.'

Sharon and Pete managed to get a council house and the troubled family moved in. 'I don't have many memories – I cut them off,' explains Sarah. 'But I do remember going into Mum's bedroom when I was four and finding her unconscious on the floor. There was a card on the phone and the emergency numbers had stars by them. My sister had taught me what to do – how to phone them and what to say. It wasn't very nice but we didn't know any other kind of life. I thought that was normal.' Sarah remembers crying as her mum's friends arrived but she doesn't recall anything else. Her survival strategy was to go into another universe in her head.

They moved to a part of the city that Sarah says was full of scallies and boy racers. In other words, it was rough, and Pete was adding to the roughness by stealing and taking drugs to perpetuate his lowlife existence. And Mum helplessly followed suite. Luckily, eight-year-old Sally looked after her sister when no one else was there. 'She's always looked out for me like a mother,' says Sarah. 'She's always been there for me no matter what, and she still is. She's always been great. She used to teach me how to look after myself – little things like how to get drinks from the fridge when I was very young.'

Just to add to their difficulties, their neighbourhood in Salford turned out to be racist. Sarah is mixed race, but refers to herself as black. 'My dad, John's, family are from Jamaica and my mum's family are from Ireland,' she says, 'and my sister and I both got bullied because we were black. Parents in our street wouldn't allow their children to play with us. I remember one boy called my sister a Paki. They were so uneducated, they didn't realise the differences between being black and Asian.'

It was oppressive and they moved again. This time their grandmother took the girls to her house. 'She didn't want Mum to look after us because it was clear she couldn't cope,' she says. 'So Grandma took us back to her house. I think Mum and Grandma had discussed it and decided that it was the best course of action for the moment. Grandma was great at getting us to school on time but we would visit Mum and Pete in the holidays.'

Sarah was in the reception class of a school, where there were only four black children, which also made her feel quite isolated. 'I got into their bad books because I hit a girl who called me a Paki,' she says. 'That was all so stupid. But I do have one good memory, which is Postman Pat coming to the school and giving us all presents.'

It was a rare moment of happiness. For the most part, trouble followed Pete around like a dark, haunting shadow. It would not go away. Someone set their car alight on their drive and, on another occasion, it was smashed to pieces in front of Sarah.

However, Sarah does have a few good memories too. 'Pete's mum lived in Wales,' she says, 'so once we went off to Wales for a day and then ended up staying a week. We played on the beach. It was great. We all enjoyed ourselves. We were all really relieved that my mother had got off a fraud charge in court, although I don't think I fully understood what was going on. We had fun together and laughed lots. That was a really good time.'

Devastating news was to greet them on their return. 'We were all smiling and in such good moods,' recalls Sarah, 'but when we got back, the house had been badly burgled and flooded. They'd emptied the place, even taking the clothes in the washing machine and the food in the fridge. It was scary – they'd ripped the radiators off the walls, which was why it flooded. The house was uninhabitable. Bad stuff followed Pete around – we didn't seem to be able to get away from it. I was always thinking, Why does this always have to happen to us? I honestly couldn't understand why life seemed so against us.' Drugs and trouble went hand in hand.

Every time they moved, they lost everything. And once again, they were destitute. 'The council tried to make us move back in,' says Sarah. 'Then they put a steel door on the house and Mum, me and Sally went to stay in a hostel. But it was like a doss house. People were taking drugs and it was a horrible environment for kids. We stayed for a few days but, when my dad found out, he went mad. He didn't want his children staying in such a disgusting place.'

John was now living with his girlfriend, Jan. He decided that he'd heard enough about the chaos and destructive behaviour that followed Pete and Sharon around. He knew his girls were at risk. So he went for custody and Sharon agreed that it was for the best. One day Sarah and Sally were met from school by their paternal grandfather. They wondered what was going on. He'd come to collect them and take them to their father's house. Sarah was six and Sally was ten.

Their new home was on the other side of town, and in more ways than one. 'It was a very different neighbourhood,' she says. 'There were trees and people looked after their gardens – it was great. We started a new school again, but this time we stayed until secondary. It was a much better place but I was still upset. I'd lost my best friend at the other school, where I was beginning to fit in at last and, however chaotic my mother was, I loved her and I really hated leaving her. But when we arrived at my dad's, I also felt a huge sense of relief. I felt safe at last.' It was also the best solution for Sarah's mother. They all hoped the arrangement would give her time and space to sort herself out.

At their dad's, there was was a big back garden to play in, plants around the house and, most importantly, they didn't have to worry all the time that their world was going to be invaded and everything was going to change dramatically. Sarah was only six and she badly needed a stable home life. 'It was so relaxing at my dad's, I could hardly believe it,' she says. 'Our primary school was totally different too. In the other one, we were the only black kids. In this one, everyone was black or Asian so there wasn't any racism to worry about.'

Sarah, Sally and their aunt went to visit their dad's family in Jamaica. It wasn't a comfortable experience for a six-year-old who had already been subject to so much upheaval in her short life. 'It scared me,' she says. 'They called us "white babies" in Kingston. It was so different to England. My granddad had chickens and goats running around his garden. I didn't like having to go to church every week. I did like the outdoor life though: the beaches and the waterfalls where you could take showers – they were so nice. But Kingston was frightening. One person gets shot there every day and that's what it felt like to me as a little girl. Granddad was building a house in a field outside Kingston and I liked that. I'm sure I'd love Jamaica if I went back now.'

Sarah was fine for the first two years at her new primary school. 'It was only five minutes from the house,' she says, 'which meant my sister and I could walk there together. It was really relaxing.'The girls also started seeing their mother again, but somehow the kids at the school found out about the drugs problem. They cruelly taunted Sarah about it. They wouldn't leave her alone and she was only eight. She was enduring experiences that you wouldn't wish on an adult.

In August 1999, the girls were out with her mother and Pete in a car. They'd visited a pawn shop and retrieved some jewellery. At a traffic light, a policeman on a motorbike spotted them and asked Pete to turn the engine off. The policeman was just walking over to check that all the papers were in order when Pete took off. 'The car was stolen and Pete didn't want the policeman to find out, so he sped off through red lights,' she explains. 'That was a fatal, split-second decision that changed all our lives. A huge lorry, which had been going through the green lights, ploughed into the side of us because the driver was distracted, as he was looking for the right road to take. We turned over seven times and our bumper flew off and chopped the policeman's leg off. It was beyond awful.'

Even worse, Sarah was conscious the entire time. She saw

exactly what happened to the policeman. She also thought her mum and her sister were dead. They were sitting next to her but very badly injured and unconscious. Both of them had to be cut out of the car. These were details that were far too much for an eight-year-old to bear. She had years of nightmares afterwards, remembering everything. Images that any adult would want to keep from a little girl. 'I couldn't see my mum's face,' she says, 'so I was frightened that she was dead. I was hardly hurt at all. Pete got out and ran off. He even tried to blend in with the crowd around the car at one point. It was so horrible, I was in shock.

'They put Sally and me in a separate hospital to our mum, so we couldn't see her and we didn't know what was going on. I hated that. Sally had to have sixty stitches in her head and some of the car's metal removed from it. I found out later that mum had broken ribs, a collapsed lung and a hole in her elbow. She was in a bad way. They kept me in hospital for a week doing check-ups. I hated it there; I hated having a nurse I didn't know supervising my bath time. My dad was really angry with my mum for letting this happen. Everything was turmoil. The one funny moment was when Sally was having an operation and dad came in with her. The staff asked if they could take out her belly-button bar, which she'd had since she was twelve. The funny thing was, Dad didn't know she had a belly-button bar, I don't think he was too pleased.'

Pete was arrested. Then the policeman died in hospital. There was no going back. 'Pete went through the lights on red,' says Sarah, 'but the lorry driver admitted that the policeman's death was his fault because he wasn't fully concentrating on the road. Pete got life for it, which was twenty-five years. We went to see him in prison once but, after that, my mum saw what a bad influence he'd been on her life and ended their relationship. The accident was a wake-up call. She realised she was messing up her life by hanging around with him. She decided that she couldn't do it any longer.'

But for all his shortcomings, Pete had been something of a father to the girls for seven years. Sarah says, 'I felt sad, even though I knew it was best for my mum to break up with him.'

The girls were so glad and so relieved when they finally got to see their mother a few weeks after the crash. They'd both been worried. 'It was Christmas and we were playing Frustration when she arrived,' says Sarah. 'It was so great to see her. She also looked really well because she'd been looked after in the hospital.'

Sarah went back to school after the car accident but suffered from flashbacks and panic attacks. Nightmares about what she had seen in the accident haunted her. Then there were newspaper reports about the accident and Pete. They culminated in Sarah enduring a hard time at school. 'Life spiralled downwards for me after the accident,' says Sarah. 'I'd see bits of the crash happening in my head and have to run out of class, crying. Then other pupils would laugh at me. I got bullied in that way. People wouldn't sit next to me or eat with me. Probably it was their parents telling them not to associate with me because of what they'd read in the newspapers, but it was horrible for me. It was more things going wrong when I needed support.'

Sarah was a lovely young girl who just needed love, care and friendship. All she seemed to get was pain and an endless stream of problems. It wasn't her fault and she had no idea what to do.

It became unbearable and she resorted to cutting herself. She was just nine years old when she discovered that self-harming could temporarily make her feel good. 'I'd go home from school, cry and cut myself. That somehow made me feel released,' she says. 'It started with compasses at school, then moved on to my dad's razors at home.'

Like many others in her situation, she was turning justifiable anger at what had happened to her back into herself. 'It became my secret pastime,' she says. 'When I saw the blood, I literally felt better. I covered up my arms so nobody suspected anything. I managed to get away with it until I was thirteen. Cutting myself provided a release – I felt relaxed afterwards.'

Sarah decided to run away from home – but not because of the emotional turmoil. Her flight came about following a vodka-drinking session with her friend, Ruby, and some boys. She had become more and more friendly with boys as her trust in girls waned. The problem was Ruby had been drinking faster than the others realised. She threw up and passed out. Sarah rang Ruby's boyfriend to ask him to take her home, which he did.

At 6am the next morning, the doorbell at Sarah's dad's home rang. Alarmingly, it was Ruby's parents. They claimed that Sarah and Ruby's boyfriend had abandoned Ruby, out of her head, in an alleyway. They were angry parents who wanted to blame someone. Sarah was scared stiff that her father would find out. She was anxious about the consequences of something that was happening to her, rather than something caused by her. This was a familiar pattern in her life.

The next day was the Muslim festival of Eid and Sarah, who hadn't told her father about the incident with Ruby, went out into town to meet up with a group of friends and have a curry with them. Her father phoned, telling her to come home immediately. He sounded angry. Sarah knew it could only be one thing: he'd found out about Ruby's false report. She was terrified about what his reaction might be. He was already blowing his top. She panicked.

She turned off her mobile phone. She also decided that she was not going to go home. She had a friend called Lynda, who had a baby and lived with her grandparents. Lynda invited her to stay. 'I didn't have any clothes on me or make-up and I really need all of that. But I was so frightened of my dad's reaction that I was willing to go without,' she says. 'I did phone Sally and tell her that I was fine. I told her to tell our dad that I wasn't coming home. Otherwise, they had no clue to where I was.'

Sarah was a reluctant runaway. She went missing but only out of fear. She thought her dad wouldn't believe her because that was her experience of him in the past. If teachers said she had misbehaved, he believed them not her. 'I was making a point,' she says. 'I was determined but I hated being away from home. I wanted to be in my own bedroom with my own clothes. I felt dirty. It was very nice of Lynda and her grandparents to have me but I would have preferred to have been at home.'

It was 14 October 2005 when Sarah ran away and she was 14. 'I'd wake up in the morning and think it was a dream,' she says. 'But it wasn't. We'd go out in town but I'd feel so stupid, having to hide in case someone saw me. It was a weird experience. I knew it wasn't me really. I wasn't the type to run away. I wanted to phone my dad but I was worried how angry he was going to be.'

She remembers getting one text from Sally, which simply

said, 'What are you doing? Everyone is worried. It's not you.' By the time she'd run away, Sarah was closer to her mum than her dad. She felt her mum did believe in her, while her dad was always arguing. After six days away, she heard a knock at the door and heard her mother's voice downstairs. 'It was so good, such a relief. It was just what I wanted to happen,' says Sarah. 'We hugged and I knew everything was fine with her. My mum left me there for another night but she gave me some of her clothes and her trainers. She drove home barefoot, that's how much she cared. I cried because, at last, it was over.'

There was only her father to be petrified of. 'I was so scared when I went back. I thought he'd go crazy but he just walked over to me and gave me an enormous hug. He also told me to forget it, but that we had to talk about problems – we mustn't hide them. He was great,' says Sarah. 'My running away was over for good. I could never handle it again.' Even Sally gave her a sisterly talking-to. 'She said if I ever needed anything, no matter what, I was to ask her and not be afraid. She offered me her unconditional support and I really appreciated that.'

Throughout the long years of uncertainty, Sarah had continued to cut herself as an escape from the emotional turmoil she felt inside. It was a transient release from pain. 'At school, I was getting bullied for doing things with boys that I wasn't doing,' she says, 'so I'd go into the toilets and self-harm. Nobody knew. I kept my sleeves long and my pain hidden.'

All that changed one evening after she'd got very drunk during a vodka session with her friends. Her father opened the door to her and he could tell she'd had too much. 'He was staring at me. I was crying and he was saying that I'd been drinking,' she says. 'We went in and I just knew that I had to get it off my chest. I'd been self-harming for four years and nobody knew. Now I had to let someone know. We sat down and I simply lifted the sleeve of my top.'

Sarah's dad took her in his arms and hugged her for a very long time until she believed that she was loved whatever she was doing to herself. No words were necessary to convey his feelings. Then he told her everything would be OK. Now that Sarah had dared to admit her self-harming, she was on the first step to recovery. 'It felt so good to tell someone,' she says. 'My dad and I grew closer and closer after that. I knew he was on my side.'

When she was 15, Sarah moved out to live with her mother. They thought they could help each other. She loved her mum and they both had problems. 'I thought she might be able to support me in a way that meant I could give up self-harming,' she says. 'And we thought I might be able to help her with her heroin addiction.'

Sarah managed to stop self-harming last year. 'I started to go to a group for self-harmers,' she explains. 'At first, I couldn't understand how it could help. A group of us sat around talking about our day-to-day lives and it all seemed a bit stupid. But we were sharing something that we all did and that was powerful. In the summertime, I was really ashamed of my arms and people looking at me as though I was strange. I started to ask myself what I was doing to my body. I started to realise that I was punishing myself for something that I wasn't responsible for.'

One morning, Sarah woke up and simply decided to stop. Amazingly, she hasn't started again. 'I still go to the group,' she says. 'People come from all sorts of different places, sometimes from really far away, and it's great to be somewhere that I'm not judged. That is brilliant.'

By the age of 16, Sarah had stopped self-harming, had started her GCSEs and was beginning to thrive. What's more, her mum gave up drugs. They were proud of one another. Not only that, Sarah could actually say she was proud of herself. That was the greatest achievement. 'Life is great in comparison to how it used to be,' she says. 'I have come through it and it feels good.'

Sarah even went on a course for gifted and talented kids at the local university and the teachers there were so impressed with her that they offered her an automatic place on a Business Studies degree course. When she later went back to visit her old school, she bumped into one of the teachers, who had never really liked her. 'She said that I was living proof that good things come to those that wait,' says Sarah, laughing.' If that teacher is acknowledging me, I really know it is true.'

For Sarah, life can only get better, and it will.

(All names in this story have been changed)

Chapter Thirteen

Your Mother and I Think About You Every Day

D erek and Diane Burns are experts in reluctant acceptance. External circumstances have forced their heads, but not their hearts, in this direction. For the last 18 years they have been living with an unimaginable reality. Their tall, good-looking, wavy-haired son, also called Derek, disappeared on 10 March 1989. They haven't heard from him since that day and nobody has seen him either. He simply vanished.

'At first we were devastated,' says Derek, 'but I still had to work and earn money. I was working hard at selling shower enclosures and I'd be travelling the country. I would always be thinking about Derek but I carried on. To be honest, that first year is a bit of a blur. I think when you are in such deep emotional pain, your mind switches off and I find it difficult to remember now. Diane kept working as a nurse. We suffered enormously. But after eighteen years, the urgency isn't the same. At some stage, we accepted that Derek was missing and that we had to live our lives. He will always be with us, we talk about him every day and I still expect him to walk through our front door one day, but we have to go on living. We realise that he would be thirty-eight if he came back now. Time hasn't stood still.'

They both derive reassurance from the fact that they hadn't argued with their son before he disappeared. Otherwise they might have blamed themselves. 'It would have been different if we'd had a row,' says Derek, 'but we hadn't. We could have understood that he might have left and not wanted to be in contact with him. But there was none of that – we were on good terms with each other. I'd even made him a cup of tea that morning in a very normal sort of way. Little was I to know that I wouldn't see him again.'

There's a steely resilience about Derek senior. He used to be in the Air Force and he's got an air of determined but cheerful rationality about him. He's caring but eminently sensible with it. Derek junior was born in Fife, in 1968. 'He was our second son,' says Derek, 'and he was a jolly wee fella. He was always laughing.' By this time, Derek had left the services and the family had moved to a new town, Glenrothes, which was near Fife.

'I became a fitter at first and we rented a house,' he says. 'Derek started school and enjoyed it there.' It wasn't long before his father got a job as a sales rep and they moved to an old house in West Calder. 'It cost £300 but we spent £1,200 doing it up. I remember, when we were moving, we had to travel over the Forth Bridge and Derek piped up, "I'm missing my friends." That made us laugh but it was also very sweet.'

Their new home was in an area redolent with history. In the late-1800s and early-1900s, Irish immigrants had moved to that part of Scotland to work in the mines and there was an emphatic division between the Catholic newcomers and the largely Protestant local community. The conflict was still going when the Burns arrived. 'I remember Derek starting primary school and running home and asking what a Catholic was,' says his father. '"Are you a Catholic?" That's the first question he'd been asked. It's changed now. People have become more adult about it, but then it was a big division.'

The Burns were a traditional nuclear family in that they ate together and enjoyed one another's company. Then five, Derek was known in the family as 'the jolly boy'. 'His grandma used to call him that,' says his father. 'He was a scamp. He wasn't naughty but he did have a twinkle in his eye.' Derek junior joined the cubs as soon as he could and he was a big fan of his brother, Gordon, who was four years older. 'He enjoyed himself when he was young,' says Derek 'He started getting involved in activities like skiing. He did very well with the school when he went to Italy. He came back with a badge to show his skill.'

The secondary school was down the road, in West Calder. 'It was quite big,' says Derek. 'There were nine hundred pupils because it had a large catchment area. At first, he did well there but that was when Gordon was also there. Derek liked hanging out with Gordon and his pals. They were all good lads and that worked out well. But in 1981, when Derek was thirteen, Gordon left school and went off to become an apprentice at an army college in Yorkshire. That was a big loss for Derek. I think he was thrown when his brother went off.'

Derek became a teenager with all the woes of the world on

his shoulders. 'He did alter,' says his father. 'He didn't seem to know what to do and the harshness of reality seemed to hit him. He wasn't smiling any more. He also started hanging out with friends that we didn't care for. He had been doing well at school but then his studies took a turn for the worse.'

By the time Derek was 15, he was playing truant from school. Not that his caring parents knew about it. 'It turned out that he'd been bunking off school for six months and we hadn't got a clue about it,' says his father. 'Him and a pal would walk up into the woods or go down into the town – they'd go anywhere but school. He'd set off for school every morning but that's not where he was going. The school didn't tell us until six months later. That would never happen these days. By that time, his school work had suffered badly and he never caught up.'

Derek has all his son's school reports. He can see the difference before and after the truancy. 'He was capable of good grades,' says his father, 'but, after bunking off school, his heart wasn't in it. It was too late; his mind had gone off education.'

Now six feet tall, Derek left school. 'He wasn't a punk but he certainly had his own style,' says his father. 'He used to wear red-and-black striped trousers. He liked the Clash. In fact, he painted one of their album covers, *Black Market Clash*, on his bedroom wall and we have left it there.'

In 1985, Derek got on to a Youth Training Scheme (YTS) in a garage. 'He loved motorbikes so this work was perfect for him,' says his father. 'And he did really well in their body shop. They liked him there and, at the end of his six month stint, the manager said he wanted to take Derek on as a proper apprentice. Derek was over the moon at this news.' It was exactly what he wanted to happen. He thought he'd found a job he liked. But the manager's boss said he didn't want to spend extra money on an apprentice when he could get away with taking on more trainees. 'He just said that he didn't need an apprentice,' he says, 'and that he would get some more YTS trainees.'

For Derek, this was earth-shattering news. Jobs are not that easy to find in West Lothian and he thought he'd found a good one. He was extremely disappointed. 'I think he was depending on that job,' says Derek senior, 'and the news that he hadn't got it blew him off his feet. He didn't cope with it very well.' Derek became disillusioned and depressed. He would skulk around in his bedroom and he didn't talk much. He still ate with the family but he wasn't very communicative. Eventually, he went to the doctor's and got himself some anti-depressants.

'He was diagnosed as depressed,' says his father. 'He was still seeing his friends but he was very sensitive and he felt very distant during this period of time. We couldn't reach him.' He managed to get himself onto another Youth Training Scheme. This time he was in a garden centre. 'He enjoyed it there,' says his father, 'but again, it didn't last long. That was the trouble with those schemes.'

In 1988, the family decided to go to Zimbabwe to visit Derek's father's brother, who was living over there. 'It was a great trip,' says Derek. 'We travelled all over the country. Derek loved it. We all got on really well, though Gordon didn't come with us because he'd been posted to Cyprus with the army.'

The only thing that Derek didn't like was that the tribal lands were being used. 'They were being stripped bare but we had to explain that the tribal people had done this for years, then they usually moved on. The trouble was, because numbers in population had increased, there were getting to be fewer and fewer places to move to. But we all had a wonderful time seeing landscapes and meeting all sorts of people. It was a great experience for all of us.'

Derek was buoyed up by his holiday for a while but, by Christmas and New Year of 1988, he had sunk back into his quagmire of misery. Over the holiday he saw his brother, whom he loved. But Gordon was also a reminder of everything that he wasn't doing. 'Gordon came home from the army on leave,' says his father, 'and I suppose it put the focus on Derek and what he wasn't doing. He must have felt that he was underachieving in everything, especially work, and he sank to his lowest point ever. But it didn't last. Afterwards, he seemed to get a new bundle of energy to do something about his life. He seemed determined to sort himself out. Diane and I were really happy about that.'

Derek cheered up. He even found himself a girlfriend in the village. He'd discovered that girls were attracted to him because of his boyish good looks. 'He went to a co-education school so he learned how to talk to girls there,' says his father. 'He would go up to them and chat.' He didn't go to nightclubs – instead a group of his friends would visit local pubs. Finding a girlfriend was another positive move.

'Kay was his first proper girlfriend,' says his father, 'and she had a job working in a local hotel. They hadn't been together long when she found another position in Hemel Hempstead. Derek seemed to have got himself out of the slough of despondency – he'd started to be his smiling self again. We were able to have a laugh. His mother and I were really pleased. One evening, he came home and he'd had a few drinks, and his friends had given him a mohican haircut. We all laughed at that, then he cut it off again. There was a good atmosphere in the house.'

All of a sudden, Derek seemed determined to find work. The evening before he disappeared, on 10 March 1989, Derek was talking to his girlfriend on the phone and his parents could hear him babbling away as they went to bed. 'I got up in the morning and I asked him if he wanted a cup of tea,' says his father. 'Then I had to go to the borders for my job, which involved a lot of travelling, so I asked him if he wanted to come. Sometimes I would take him with me when he was unemployed. That day was rainy and miserable. Derek said he didn't want to come and mentioned that he might pop down to Edinburgh. With that, I went out into the rain. It was so normal, it's shocking – I didn't see him after that.'

There was no disagreement. As a family, they were all getting on well. Derek and Diane are keen to point out that there was no black cloud hanging over their relationship with their son. There was no reasonable explanation for what happened next.

By 6pm, the normally reliable Derek had not turned up for his evening meal. His parents weren't unduly worried. He was a 19-year-old adult and they weren't keeping tabs on him. 'On the other hand, he would normally phone us to let us know what he was doing,' says his father. 'But we weren't perturbed. We went to bed at 10.30pm and he still wasn't in, and I suppose we thought he must be out drinking with his pals.'

The next morning, Derek had still not returned. His bedroom was empty. His mess lay undisturbed. His father had to go off to Aberdeen that day but the parents were starting to worry. His mother rang around his friends but nobody knew where Derek was. The couple were totally confused and they were taking his disappearance seriously. His mother rang the police. They noted that he had gone missing but they weren't proactive. 'The trouble was Derek was an adult of nineteen,' says Derek, 'so they concluded that he had left of his own free will and that there was nothing they could do about it.' Back in 1989, there was no separate police unit for missing people. 'It would have been different if he'd been underage or if he'd been threatened,' says his father. 'Then the police would have acted. As it was, we felt helpless and powerless. It was a terrible time for us.'

Derek was a homeboy and his parents couldn't imagine that he had voluntarily left them without saying anything. 'That threw us,' says his father. 'It was completely out of character. We were worried sick but we didn't know what to do.'

Gradually, as the first few days passed following his disappearance, they pieced together something of a story. Derek, it transpired, had gone to Edinburgh with some friends and had a few drinks that fateful day. Still in the frame of mind where he was thinking positively about getting work, and encouraged by the alcohol, it seemed he had decided that he would go and visit his girlfriend. He also thought he would ask about work at the same hotel. Derek caught the bus down to Hemel Hempstead, found the hotel and had a cup of tea with Kay. But his idea that he might find a job at the same hotel as her was foiled. The manager told him there was no work. Derek left, defeated, telling Kay he'd better get the bus home.

He never reached the bus, much less home. Derek simply disappeared into thin air. There have been no positive sightings of him since he was at the hotel. For 18 years, his mystified parents have wondered what on earth happened to him. Did he decide to go into the city and look for work there? Did he meet someone who offered him work? He hadn't got his passport or his savings book with him, so did he assume another identity? Was he murdered by a stranger? Did he have a terrible accident? All these horrendous possibilities have plagued them at one time or another.

Not ones to sit and do nothing, Derek and Diane went to try and get Kay's phone number from her parents, only to find they relied on their daughter calling them. They didn't know the name of the hotel in Hemel Hempstead either. 'We live a long way away from there,' says Derek's father. 'And, unfortunately, we never got to speak to Kay, because she died from a drugs-related incident not long afterwards. That seems very strange, but it is true.'

Thwarted in their attempts to see his girlfriend, his parents turned their attention to a couple of boys from the village, who had moved to a squat in Battersea. 'We decided to go and visit to see if Derek had gone there,' says his father. 'We got there and saw some youngsters playing football in the back. Diane immediately thought she saw Derek but it wasn't him. They didn't know where he was and hadn't seen him. One of them led us away from the squat. I think they were embarrassed by the state of it and probably by what was happening inside.'

They also went to the headquarters of the Salvation Army in London. 'They tried to find him for about a month, then rang to say they couldn't do any more,' says Derek. Nothing that had happened made any sense to the couple. Derek was the sort of lad who would ring them if he found himself short of cash. There were few organisations offering support to families of the missing at that time and the couple felt alone in their search for their son. They tried checking with the DHSS and the Inland Revenue to see if he was registered, but came up against a brick wall. They put adverts in a motorbike magazine that Derek always bought and in *Exchange and Mart* but still they didn't discover anything.

'You always feel like you should be doing more,' says Derek's father, 'but we didn't know what. London is so big, it would be like looking for a needle in a haystack. We did everything that we could logically do. It is terrible, but in the end you start accepting that your son is missing and there is nothing that you can do. It takes a lot of getting used to. The thoughts about him never go away but you do learn to deal with it.'

Derek's father talks about the disappearance of his son as a sort of death. 'It feels like he's died, even if we hope that he is out there somewhere still alive. He is not in our lives in any way that doesn't make it feel like death and our feelings are very similar to parents whose children have died. But it's worse because we don't know what has happened to him. If we knew Derek had died, at least we would be able to understand why he was missing. At the moment, his disappearance defies logic and that is very difficult. It's also very hard to die in the UK and not be found. That's another bit of confusing rationality that makes Derek's disappearance challenging.'

Some 18 years later, they have had Derek's case highlighted in the *Big Issue*, they've done interviews in the press and on the radio, and the police even started working on his file again a couple of years ago. Derek travelled down to Bournemouth and to Hereford, both places where his son was reported to be working in motorbike shops but, sadly, he didn't find him.

There was a false sighting of him in Sterling but, ultimately, they still have no idea what happened. They considered going to see clairvoyants but dismissed the idea as clutching at straws.

'In the end, you have to deal with the situation yourself,' says Derek's father. 'We have exhausted all the possibilities at the moment. We still hope that our son will walk in one day out of the blue but, in the meantime, we haven't kept his room the same. We've packed away his clothes but they are still there in boxes. In the end, you have to let go a little and get on with your lives. We are still thinking positively about him but we're no longer buying Christmas and birthday presents for him. We talk about him and ask questions like, "I wonder if he's married and got children?" We don't let him disappear from our minds and hearts, but we have also learned, over a long period of time, how to carry on living our lives.'

Derek and Diane have the memory of their son with them and they never stop hoping that he will turn up again one day – but neither do they expect it. There's a subtle difference and that's what their acceptance that Derek is missing has brought them. 'It never goes away,' says Derek's father. 'It's like emotional toothache, but we have confronted it. It doesn't mean that we don't miss him every day.'

Chapter Fourteen

I Was Reunited with My Mother and We Are So Alike

Claire Lee is a mixed-race, curvaceous, curly-haired, 37-year -old mother of five. She lives in Kennington, in South London, with her sweet, loving, Rastafarian partner, Jerome. Claire is a vibrant, courageous woman, who grew up with only two memories of her mother.

'Mum left home when I was three so I remember very little about her then,' says Claire. 'But I do have a memory of the flat in Acton and seeing my mum opening the door to Father Christmas. The hall was full of presents. The other memory is of sitting watching *Top of the Pops* with her and eating fish and chips. It was weird growing up with so few memories to hold on to in my head.'

These were very small but treasured memories. When her mother, Kathleen, left, her stepfather, William, adopted Claire, but forbade any mention of her mother in the house. She was brutally expunged from their existence – there was no trace of her left. 'There were no clothes, no photographs and I wasn't allowed to talk about her,' she says. 'She simply disappeared from our lives without explanation. I remember Dad banging the fridge, shouting and going crazy but that's about it. I didn't really understand. For me as a child, mum just left and I have no recollection of how I felt. As I got older, I blocked out any feelings of sadness and guilt, and focused on surviving. "Mum" was a taboo word in the house. She didn't exist.'

Claire had a little sister, Sarah, who was just a one-year-old when their mother left home. 'She has no memories at all of Mum, which is sad,' says Claire. 'And she is still very angry about that period of her life. She felt abandoned.' Claire's birth father was absent too. Much later, she found out he had come from Barbados and left her mother when she was five months pregnant. He has never been in contact with any of them since. 'He obviously couldn't handle being a father,' says Claire, pragmatically, adding that she has never had any real desire to find him because he never showed any interest in her. But as she grew up, she thought she understood why her mother had left their household.

As a child, Claire felt rootless and lost. She had no real idea of identity. Her mother was white and Scottish, her birth father was from Barbados and her stepdad was from Montserrat. 'I just played around with different identities at school,' she says. 'When I was friendly with a girl whose family was from Jamaica, I'd become Jamaican. If they were from Trinidad, I'd become Trinidadian. I didn't know who I was. It was hard for me not really knowing where I came from. At that point, I didn't know the origins of my mother or my father, only my stepdad.'

The three of them of them lived in a little block of low-rise flats in Acton. Their stepdad worked in a local ice-cream factory, spent a lot of time in the betting shop and was very strict. Claire says she felt like a modern-day Cinderella, doing all the cooking and cleaning. She was forced to be a little mother at home to her sister. 'I could go out to play but I had to be in by curfew time or I'd get hit.'

The beatings from her stepdad started when she was six or seven. They didn't stop until Claire escaped from home. 'It was as though he despised the sight of me,' she says. 'I look like my mother, so he resented having me there because seeing me must have been like looking at my mother. My sister didn't get the same treatment. She didn't look so much like Mum. Sarah was treated like a little princess, whereas I was always in the wrong and he'd lash out at me. I always hoped my sister would jump in and help me but she didn't because our stepdad was very scary and dominant. It made me sad that he always came across as being very bitter about women and life. It was a horrible childhood with him. Knowing that someone doesn't want you around doesn't make for great self-confidence.'

In the evening, William would invite friends or one of his many girlfriends to the flat. On those occasions the girls would be told to go to their bedroom. 'We'd peep out and see they were drinking and watching porn films,' she says. 'I'm sure they were doing other adult things afterwards. He was a womaniser so he would have a lot of different women coming round.'

Claire was taunted at junior school for not having a mother, making school life unbearable too. 'Dad actually had a long-term partner for a few years, called Gill, who also had a couple of kids. They are like my brothers and sisters now. She was great,' says Claire. 'She actually came to school at break, specifically so that I could call out, "Hi, Mum," and stop those kids from tormenting me. Gill really supported me and was like a mum, but she wasn't around when my dad was violent. It wasn't easy for her. I also went through periods when I was resentful and angry that my real mother wasn't around. I hated having nothing of my real mum around – well, in the end, I found one platform shoe. That was the sum total of the possessions that she left behind.'

Claire was also cruelly called 'Claire Flea' at school because all her clothes came from jumble sales. There was one particularly painful occasion when Claire turned up to school unknowingly wearing clothes that had been donated by one of the other girls there. 'I felt such a tramp,' she says, 'and so rejected. It was very tough. I had no idea either how to be girly or do my hair in a pretty way. I didn't have that kind of a role model, even when Gill was around for a few years.'

Her stepdad began to hit her more and more violently and, by the time she was 11, she started to understand why her mother had left. It seemed so wrong for a mother to leave her children, but there was an explanation and Claire was working it out. 'It became obvious to me that he'd been brutal to her and beaten her up,' she says. 'I really started to get a picture of how cruel he had been to her so I started to understand why she would have had to get away from him. She would have been saving her life.'

Finally, Claire told social services that she was being beaten by her stepdad, but they came round and he charmed them. Nothing happened. She lost faith in the system. There was no one to help her when she desperately needed it. Not surprisingly, Claire became an insecure teenager who found it hard to trust adults. Although intelligent, she turned into a problem student because she'd been treated so badly at home and at school. Like many in such vicious circles of behaviour, Claire turned into a bully herself. She also badmouthed teachers and generally behaved in a disruptive manner or acted as the classroom clown in order to get attention. Claire had found out how to get her own back on the world for the background of abuse she had suffered. If she didn't have any self-esteem, she'd find a performance of it in herself instead.

But there was one class that Claire excelled in – English. She used her essays as a therapeutic outlet, although she didn't realise that was what she was doing. 'Our teacher asked us to write an essay about our life experiences,' she says. 'So she received a hundred pages from me containing all the agony of my existence at home. This English teacher was called Miss Spivey and she was a godsend to me. She read it all and really understood what was happening to me. After that, she gave me a lot of special treatment, which really made a difference to my life. She would take me out for lunch and praise my work. Miss Spivey was fantastic and I would have loved it if she'd been able to foster me. I could talk to her properly so that was great for me and it meant someone knew what was going on. That was really important too.'

Through Miss Spivey, Claire was sent to the Child Guidance Centre. It was a well-meant move but all the supportive work was undone because everything Claire said about the violent relationship with her father was reported back to him. 'I told them at first what was really happening to me at home,' she says, 'but they told my stepdad. So that didn't work and it meant I clammed up altogether.'

Over the years, Claire thought about her mum more and more, and fantasised about getting in touch with her, meeting her, being with her. When she was 15, she wrote to the Salvation Army and requested that they look for her mother. But she didn't know her mother's date of birth and didn't get an answer. She felt powerless but she wanted to find her mum so much.

Her stepfather continued his brutality, culminating in an outburst that was to change her life. 'I went round to my friend Chloe's house and they had some potato wine they'd made themselves,' she says, 'which they wanted me to taste. I had a tiny amount but when I got home, my stepdad came back from the pub with a couple of friends. I'd eaten some polo mints and I'd only had a tiny amount of this potato wine, but he managed to smell alcohol on my breath. He launched into a physical attack on me, hit me hard and threw things at me. It was really terrible this time and I decided to leave. I'd had enough of this life with him and his anger.'

Intimidated by his size and volatility, Claire let him fall asleep in the chair and left. For ever. First of all, she went round to a friend of her dad who she called Uncle Pete, just to let someone know where she was. Then she rang her social worker. 'She told me I was sixteen now and the police couldn't force me to go home. I even went with her back to our family flat because I'd left with nothing, and she explained to him that I wanted to pick up some clothes and my school work. He let us in but he refused to let us leave.'

Her stepdad attacked Claire and her social worker. 'He went

for me,' she says. 'Sue jumped in to try to stop him and he lashed out at her. He hit me in the stomach a few times but then we managed to get away. This social worker, Sue, was in tears afterwards. She was crying and saying sorry to me – she knew I felt let down.'

As the incident had been witnessed, the social services went into action. 'They sent me to a children's home in Greenford,' says Claire. 'And, in fact, there were some fantastic staff who genuinely looked after me and loved me. It was incredible. I loved it.' Unfortunately, Claire was too old at 16 to stay in a children's home and, after 2 months, they put her into lodgings with foster carers. 'The first ones were in Greenford and the mother was a black lady who really wanted me to call her "Mum", but I didn't want anyone else except for my mother to be my mum. So that didn't work out. She was too overbearing.'

The next move was much more successful. Claire stayed with a couple called Sharon and Tony in their huge house with a lovely garden, in Sudbury Hill. They were also very kind to her. This was her dream come true. 'I spent a year with them,' she says, 'and they really did help to pick me up. They were great to me.'

But there was trouble brewing in the shape of Johnny, a 16-year-old bad boy whom she'd met at the children's home. 'I wasn't promiscuous in my teens but I did revel in the attention from boys,' she says. 'It made me feel good and, because my self-esteem was so low, I felt as though I needed it. But I had a problem in that I didn't know how to distinguish sex and love. I craved love because I hadn't had enough of it, but I mixed it up with sex. I thought sex was love. I guess this attitude was also learned from my dad and all his womanising. But it spelled horror for my relationships with boys.'

They were a mirror for one another. Johnny, like Claire, was the black sheep of his family. But he was also out of control. His mother didn't know how to deal with him. He ran roughshod over everyone. 'He was bringing me gifts like radios and hairdryers,' says Claire. 'I thought it was great. I thought, This is a man who loves me.' So she had sex with him but realised that neither of them really understood love. They hadn't learned those vital lessons from their families.

Despite her lack of sexual knowledge, Claire admits that she liked to act as though she knew it all. 'I let him think I was the "Queen of the *Kama Sutra*",' she says. 'I put on a mask and acted. I also had a very effective mask in life, which sent out the message "Don't mess with Claire". That was very useful and I never let the real Claire out. That was my safety helmet. In sex, I'd act as though I knew what was going on, but underneath I didn't have a clue. I thought sex was love so everything would be fine.'

Not surprisingly, it wasn't. Claire became pregnant at 16. 'I was going to my sixth-form classes pregnant and trying to catch up on my GCSEs, which I'd missed because I was having an unstable home life,' says Claire. 'I was actually glad to be pregnant at that time, because my dreams were all about having the baby of the man I loved. And I thought that was Johnny.'

Claire spent all her spare time at the house Johnny shared with his mother in Acton. But Johnny's behaviour was impossible. 'His mother was dominated by him. She let him get away with murder,' says Claire.

Claire gave birth to her first baby, Sabrina, and she was happy.

Except when Johnny came to the hospital, had a look in the cot and said, 'What a funny-looking mutt.' Claire was horrified that he could react to his daughter in that way. And that was only the beginning.

Back at the house, Johnny's mother tried to take over looking after baby Sabrina. Claire wasn't willing to put up with anyone else curbing her freedom so she moved back into a flat that had previously been allocated to her by the council. By some strange twist of fate, this was the very place in which she'd grown up with her stepfather and sister. History was going to repeat itself for Claire, her baby and Johnny. Claire was just 17.

In another weird but portentous coincidence, Claire had only just moved back in when a letter arrived that had been re-addressed to Kathleen Lee – her mother. The original address was in Chiswick, also in London. Understandably, Claire had a surge of feelings about her mother and thought again about finding her. The letter seemed to be a sign that she should go to west London. She turned up at the house, expecting her mother to answer the door. A man answered it and Claire demanded, 'Where's my mother?' Sadly, he had no idea who her mother was or where she was.

Claire was then filled with fresh determination to find her mother. She sent letters to the police and the Salvation Army, all to no avail. She still didn't have her mother's date of birth. She also wrote to Cilla Black to try and get on *Surprise, Surprise*, to *Trisha* and to Robert Kilroy-Silk. 'The *Kilroy* programme phoned me,' she says, 'but they wanted me to go on and talk about why I hated my mother for leaving, and I couldn't do that. I didn't feel hate for her. I just wanted to appeal for my mother to come forward. I desperately wanted to find her.'

In the meantime, despite a deteriorating relationship with Johnny, Claire got pregnant again, this time with a son who would be called Junior. She was still only 18. It made no difference to her relationship with Johnny. He wanted to possess Claire completely and deny her any freedom. She put up with far more than she should have done because she'd never learned how to look after herself in that kind of situation.

'I decided I'd had enough of Johhny and I met someone else called John, who treated me like a princess. He was a charming, lovely man but I was to discover he was also weak.' Now Claire had two children, a tough ex-boyfriend and a new boyfriend.

She was soon pregnant by John with a daughter, who would be called Zoe. Claire was 20 and she had an awful lot on her plate. What's more, her new boyfriend wouldn't stand up to Johnny, despite being six feet, two inches tall. Johnny couldn't bear having a child around who wasn't his and the sight of her would provoke him. Claire coped by giving Zoe to the neighbours for a while if she knew Johnny was coming. The new boyfriend didn't last long.

Claire became determined to get away from Johnny. Now she wanted him out of her life for good, but she knew he would keep coming back to the flat. 'The police found me and the kids a house in Ealing Common. We didn't take anything with us,' she says. 'It was a bit like when I left home when I was sixteen. Eventually, social services found us a women's refuge in Clapham Common.

The family stayed at the refuge for nearly a year. Claire says it was a wake-up call for her. 'I really saw how women were being seriously abused by men,' she says. 'It makes me shudder to think of some of the ways women had been hurt. It disgusted me that men could do that. There was one nineteen-year-old black girl who'd been cut from her neck to her belly and across her chest like a cross. This experience really opened my eyes. But we were like one big family in there as well. There was a lot of generosity and shared times, which were wonderful.'

Claire also had time to think again about her mother and finding her. She talked to her social worker and, eventually, she was invited to Acton Town Hall so that social services could set about searching for her file, which would include information about her adoption. It was locked away in a vault somewhere and it took weeks to turn up. Finding it wasn't the end of the story. 'It was very frustrating,' Claire says, 'as certain bits of information was missing or blocked out because of the Adoption Act. This included my mother's date of birth, which was what I really needed to start a search for her.'

The file included disturbing bits of information about her school days, which took her straight back to her stepfather's abuse. 'I wouldn't do PE because it was too shameful. My back was black and blue and I didn't want the other kids to see it,' she says, 'so I'd get into trouble for not doing that lesson. Then there was one occasion, when a teacher had been annoyed with me. She lifted my shirt. She gasped very loudly in shock. "Do you want to talk about this?" she asked. That's when social services were called in, when I was fifteen. But I'd just get hit again after my stepdad had been seen by them.' There were painful memories in these reports, but there was no real help in finding her mother.

It was another 13 years and another 2 babies, Naomi and Nya, before Claire was able to focus on the task of looking for her mother. Claire and her family were eventually given a large council flat in Kennington, by which time she had found a steady man in her partner, Jerome. All her children had known about her desire to find her mother, but somehow it never actually happened. She was too busy looking after them.

But a newly determined Claire contacted social services again in 2005. This time, she and her social worker actually went to Somerset House to search for her mother's date of birth. 'I knew she was about fifty-six because Gill and her were around the same age,' says Claire. 'We searched through dozens of books and we found the marriage certificate but there were no details of Mum's date of birth. As a last desperate measure, we decided that it would be worth applying to the court for the original adoption papers because my stepfather had adopted me when I was three'

Another few months passed before a letter came back with the age and date of birth of Claire's mother. It also confirmed that her father was from Barbados. At last, after all these years, Claire had the vital piece of information that made it possible to find her mother. 'I was really excited,' she says. 'I knew now I was getting nearer to her. In November 2005, I sent off a letter to the Salvation Army again.'

Five months later, she received a phone call. 'I was convinced that my mother wouldn't have retained the surname Lee after the way my stepdad had treated her, so I had asked the Salvation Army to look under her maiden name, which was Eavemen. However, they couldn't find her, so they said they'd have a go with Lee,' Claire explains. 'I was phoning them about four times a week, I was so desperate to find my mum.'

With that surname, they traced her mother the same day.

Claire was actually on her way to Peckham to buy some chicken when she received that momentous call on her mobile. 'I thought it was a debt collector.' She laughed. 'But it was a Salvation Army major asking me it if I was able to talk. He told me he'd just come off the phone to my mother.' Claire nearly fell over in the road. She whooped with joy and she skipped all the way to Peckham. 'I had such strong feelings,' she says. 'It was like being at the fairground. Sadness and joy were tumbling around my body all at the same time, but I was also experiencing surges of excitement. The end was in sight – my mother was getting nearer to me.'

The Salvation Army usually advise people to correspond before they actually meet so that there is a gentle build-up to the emotional encounter. Letters – long, explanatory, loving letters – passed between Claire and her mother for four weeks.

'Then I couldn't stand it any longer,' says Claire. 'I could feel her through her letters. It was great but now I wanted us to meet. We'd already explained everything to each other. She told me why she'd left my stepfather and it was what I'd thought all along. He'd been violent to her and she'd had to escape. The truth was, she wasn't in her right mind. Mum had a mental breakdown. She couldn't cope; she didn't think she was capable of looking after Sarah and me. He was so brutal to her that she ended up in a women's refuge, just like me. Then, when she got better, she thought her daughters might not want to know her and that perhaps it was better for us if she stayed away. We'd explained so much to each other that we agreed it was time for us to actually meet.'

On 14 May 2005, Claire and her long-lost, much-loved mother arranged to meet at Marble Arch tube station. Claire was in an extreme state of anticipation and excitement. After all, this was a moment she had waited 35 years for. 'I got off the bus and decided I'd try to take a peep at who I thought she was, rather than be directly confronted by her,' admits Claire. 'There was a lady dressed in black standing underneath some scaffolding and my heart was telling me it was her. I said, "Hello," and we ended up having a hug that made us look like we were a couple of lesbians. It was such an incredible feeling for both of us.'

Claire and Kathleen went off to a coffee bar nearby. They simply talked and talked. Years and years of missed words filled the hours. Thankfully, mother and daughter bonded despite their years apart. There was no question of them not getting on. 'We are so similar,' says Claire. 'Mum's Scottish and white, I'm mixed race, but we have the same nose, the same shape eyes, the same thin upper lip and, most of all, we're both driven by our feelings. It was like meeting with a part of me that I always knew was there but had never been able to reach. It was such a brilliant affirmation of who I am. So often I'd been under-confident. Now suddenly I felt like I could be all of myself.'

They were so entwined with one another that they didn't want to leave. Claire suggested that her mum – who lives in Leytonstone – could come and visit her house then and there. Kathleen agreed. 'We were greeted in Kennington by all my five kids, who broke into rapturous applause as we entered,' says Claire proudly. 'They all knew how long I'd been looking for my mum. Everyone gelled immediately and it was heaven. This was the final bit of my family jigsaw puzzle to be put in place. I'd already found a sweet man in Jerome. Now I had my mother back too.'

Friends often remark how alike Claire and her mother are. Kathleen has the ability to tune into her daughter's feelings. 'She'll ask me how I'm feeling and I'll say, "I'm fine,"' says Claire, 'and she'll say, "No, you're not," and she's absolutely right. We're like two peas in a pod. I'm so happy to have found her and she feels the same way. Now we see each other all the time.'

Strangely enough, around the same time that she found her mother, her stepfather had a stroke. She had still had some contact with him because her sister Sarah had continued to live with him. Claire felt a mixture of euphoria about finding her mother and unexpected grief about her stepfather's fragility. 'I went to see him in hospital and he couldn't speak,' she says. 'And at one point, he looked at me straight in the eyes and burst into tears. My stepfather never cried but here he was, the shadow of his former self and vulnerable at last. I understood that those tears represented all the pain he had caused me and they were all the apologies that he couldn't actually speak. At that moment, I felt care and love for this person whom I had despised for so long. It was a cathartic moment.'

Her stepfather even recovered for a while. 'He started talking again. He went home and I'd buy him fish from the market,' she says. 'I could see in his eyes that he was sorry for everything he'd done to me, but he could never bring himself to actually say it.' The recovery was short lived and it was only a few months later that he died.

This wasn't an easy period for Claire. She was in agony and ecstasy at the same time. She was dealing with a lot of strong feelings that arose from her childhood. Her stepfather dying had brought up all the feelings of fear and rejection she'd repressed when he was beating her. Claire had found her mother, which was a source of happiness, but also sadness in that it reminded her of all the lost time between them. 'I felt as though I was on a rollercoaster,' says Claire. 'Then I broke my ankle, which forced me to stop and stay in. Something physical had to break because so much was being churned up emotionally inside by these dramatic events.'

She went through 18 months during which her past came back to haunt her in all its full-blown misery and, to deal with it, she went first to a group that focused on anxiety and then she attended one on depression. They helped put her feelings into perspective. 'Mum could relate to it. She helped me come through,' she says. 'I went to stay with her a lot during this time. I was in a super-sensitive state. Mum's love and advice pulled me through.'

In the two years since mother and daughter were reunited, Claire's life was transformed. Kathleen would come down to Kennington every other weekend. Claire would go up to see her once a week. They went shopping together. They loved eating together. They'd sit by the river and chat. Claire was in the best place she'd ever been in her life. 'I feel strong and optimistic,' she says. 'I'm a very spiritual person and I'm a talker too. I wanted it for so long. It's just so brilliant that my relationship with her is better than even I could have imagined.'

To celebrate the second anniversary of their reunion, they went on holiday to Barbados together. Claire's dream came true. Her mum was missing, but not any longer.

Epilogue

As I finish this book, images of missing four-year-old Madeleine McCann have recently been filling our screens and newspapers, our hearts and minds. As are those of her parents, looking exhausted and anguished but determined to find her. Unimaginably, they were then cast as suspects themselves and headlines across the world accused them of her murder.

Madeleine's enchanting presence, with her long, blonde hair, innocent smile and her distinctive, black iris-flash in her right eye, has been radiating out to us via the posters all over Europe and on the internet. It's hard to imagine anyone in the UK not being aware that Madeleine is missing. Over 100 million people have visited her website. There have been more media stories about her case than any other I can think of. I'm very aware from writing this book that the majority of children and adults who go missing do not get this kind of coverage. However, the relatives left behind have all had similar feelings to those of the McCanns.

The almost unspeakable horror is that Madeleine's parents – and the rest of us by proxy through the media – do not know what the outcome will be. 'A stolen child evokes ancient terrors,' wrote Howard Jacobson in the *Independent*. 'Not for nothing do fairy stories abound of tales of lost and abandoned children, as though we dare only glimpse through the refracted light of myth our capacity to do children harm and even suspect we half-hope for what we dread.' Certainly, the media plays on this aspect in the daily drama of Madeleine's disappearance.

In this book, the families who have missing loved ones – whether they have disappeared abroad or at home or walked out on their families – may not have had the global spotlight upon them. They, and the relatives of the other 600 people that go missing in the UK every day, have still all suffered from this awful uncertainty. When someone is missing, it is in some ways like a death, but it isn't. It's like a death without the body and it's this not knowing that is the most unbearable.

Time and time again, I interviewed mothers, brothers, wives, fathers and sisters who vacillated between despair and hope. It seems to be the ghastly lot of those who are left behind. 'There's an essential ambiguity to having someone missing,' says counsellor, author and spokesperson for the British Association for Counselling and Psychotherapy, Phillip Hodgson. 'There is no resolution, there is no body, so these people are in limbo. They travel between the torture of hope and anguish. They are forced to be in two places at the same time, which is very hard for human beings.

'In some ways, their identity is being challenged – are they a mother still if their son is missing? On the other hand, they want to remain full of hope because the alternative, of possible murder, is unthinkable to them. Those who have missing parents go through similar feelings. There is the not knowing about their own identities until they find their missing parent.'

Fortunately, all the sons and daughters I interviewed for this book have found the parents missing through divorce or adoption. They experienced the joy of reunion within themselves, as well as with their parents. There are also one or two fortunate instances in which a missing husband and runaway daughter are found. However, the remaining relatives are condemned to the nightmare of uncertainty.

'It would be so much easier if we were computers,' says Phillip Hodson, 'but we feel grief, anger and, sometimes, guilt.' Different people react in different ways. Jo Gibson Clark and Nicki Durbin, who both have missing sons, are still out there on a brave crusade to find out what has happened to their lovely sons. Others have accepted – often because their loved ones have been gone longer – that there's nothing they can do. They still hope and even expect to see them again, but they have accepted that have done everything they can.

Derek Burns has been missing for 18 years and his father says, 'At some stage, we accepted that Derek was missing and that we had to live our lives. He will always be with us. We talk about him every day and I still expect him to walk through our front door one day, but we have to go on living. He disappeared when he was nineteen, but we realise he would be thirty-eight if he comes back now. Time hasn't stood still.'

There are no clear cut, emotional stages that relatives of missing people go through. 'They don't go from one door to the next,' says Phillip Hodson. 'It's more like a complicated version of the grieving process. It is like bereavement but without the closure.' Shock, anger, guilt, devastation, depression and sadness – they are all emotions that can be evoked by having a missing loved one. 'Initially, it's important that people find emotionally intelligent support. It's wise to choose who they are,' says psychotherapist and author of *Courage To Love*, Malcolm Stern. 'And it's good to find support from people who can be with their feelings, so they don't encourage you to repress yours.'

Talking to other families that are in the same predicament can be immensely valuable. Lee Boxell's mother, Christine – he went missing 18 years ago – found great comfort in discussing everything about Lee and what may have happened to him with other families in the same situation. Nicki Durbin also mentioned how useful she found discussing the bleaker parts of what she has imagined around her missing son, Luke.

If years pass – and this is quite possible – and a relative is still missing, it's clearly important for people to allow themselves to live their lives again. This may include being present and active around the rest of their family. 'There comes a time,' says Phillip Hodson, 'and it will be different for everyone, when the focus has to change away from being exclusively on the missing person and back on to the rest of your family.'

Everyone wants to keep the memory of their missing one alive and vibrant. Inventing rituals to remember or having a dedicated shrine in the house or garden can be helpful. Rebecca Carr's mother, Lynne, has planted two pink Rebecca roses in her garden and made a collage of photos for Rebecca's eight-year-old son, Tyler. The Burns keep the memory of their son Derek alive through keeping a wall painting he did of an album cover by The Clash. Psychotherapist Macolm Stern suggests a weekly meditation focusing on the missing may be useful. 'You could gather together as a family every week,' he says, 'and sit quietly remembering your missing one. That could be a very spiritually rich place to remember them.'

The truth is there isn't an easy-to-follow map for families with missing loved ones. The path is painful, whichever way they choose. I can only continue to salute their courage.

Resources and
Helplines

Missing People

Formerly known as the National Missing Persons Helpline, this is the UK's only charity working with young runaways, missing and unindentified people, their families and others that care for them. As well as actively searching for missing people and supporting those who are trying to find them, Missing People offers three other services: Runaway Helpline, Message Home and Identification. All Missing People's Services are free of charge.

Main helpline
Freefone 0500 700 700
If calling from abroad, it is 00 44 20 8392 4545
www.missingpeople.org.uk

Runaway Helpline is for young people seeking confidential help
Freefone 0808 800 7070
www.runawayhelpline@missingpeople.org.uk

Message Home is a confidential service offering help, advice and support to adults who are missing. It is available 24 hours a day and 7 days a week

Freefone 0800 700 740

messagehome@missingpeople.org.uk

The Salvation Army

They offer a family tracing service for adult members of family when contact has been lost, whether recently or in the distant past. It operates in a hundred countries around the world. Every day of the year, ten people are reunited with their family in the UK alone. They will not trace adopted children, fathers of children born outside marriage, friends or family history.

Main contact number – 020 7367 4747 Monday to Friday, 8.15am–3.45pm

www.salvationarmy.org

Enquiries directly to:

The Salvation Army, Family Tracing Service, 101 Newington Causeway, London SE1 6 BN

The Children's Society

This is a national children's charity established in 1881, working with 50,000 children and teenagers every year. It is driven by the belief that every child deserves a good childhood. It provides vital help and understanding for those forgotten children who face the greatest danger, discrimination or disadvantage: children who are unable to find the support they need anywhere else. The charity supports children at risk on the streets, children in trouble with the law and children with disabilities.

Main contact number – 0207 7841 4423
www.childrenssociety.org.uk

Self-Harm
www.nshn.co.uk links you to the National Self-Harm
Network.
You can email info@nshn.co.uk
You can read about self-harm on http://www.nhsdirect.nhs.uk
You can also call Childline on 0800 1111

Other Useful Internet Sites
www.look4them.org gives useful information for those
looking for missing people, for those searching for missing
relatives and those who may have had children abducted.

www.missing-people.co.uk provides a free appeals service for
those seeking missing people, including friends and family.

www.mispers.com is a worldwide service for missing people,
but only those who have a recognised police force conducting
an investigation into their case. It does not provide search
services.

www.missingkids.co.uk is a police website dedicated to finding
missing and abducted children.